FISHING AND THINKING

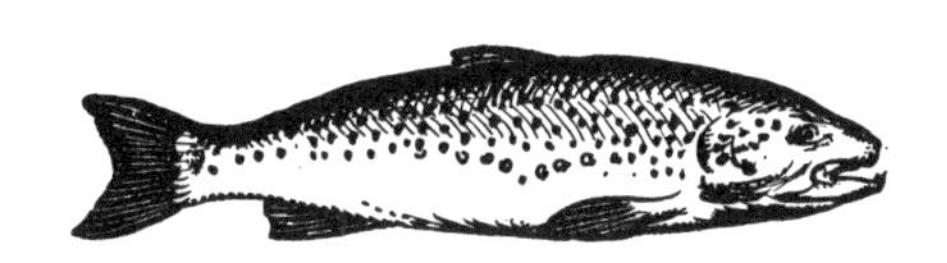

FISHING AND THINKING

A. A. LUCE

WITH A FOREWORD BY DATUS PROPER

RAGGED MOUNTAIN PRESS
CAMDEN, MAINE

Published by Ragged Mountain Press, an imprint of TAB Books. TAB Books is a division of McGraw-Hill, Inc.

First published in Great Britain in 1959 by Hodder and Stoughton Ltd. A facsimile edition with a new introduction was published in Great Britain in 1990 by Swan Hill Press, an imprint of Airlife Publishing.

10 9 8 7 6 5 4 3 2 1

Library of Congress Cataloging -in-Publication Data
Luce, A. A. (Arthur Aston), 1882-
Fishing and thinking / A.A. Luce
p. cm.
Originally published: London : Hodder and Stoughton, 1959.
ISBN 0-87742-400-4
1. Fishing—Ireland. I. Title.
SH612.L83 1993
799.1'2'09415—dc20 93-15049
CIP

Questions regarding the content of this book should be addressed to:
Ragged Mountain Press
P.O. Box 220
Camden, ME 04843

Questions regarding the ordering of this book should be addressed to:
TAB Books, A Division of McGraw-Hill, Inc.
Blue Ridge Summit, PA 17294
1-800-233-1128

A portion of the profits from the sale of each Ragged Mountain Press book is donated to an environmental cause.

Fishing and Thinking is printed on 60-pound Renew Opaque Vellum, an acid-free paper that contains 50 percent recycled waste paper (preconsumer) and 10 percent postconsumer waste paper.
Printed by R.R. Donnelley, Crawfordsville, Indiana.
Production by Molly Mulhern.

CONTENTS

FOREWORD

An American Guide to *Fishing and Thinking*

EVERY good book is an act of love, a flow of passion into pages, and every author wants the love requited. Imagine, then, the courage it must have taken for A. A. Luce to link fishing and thinking in his title, knowing that some thinkers do not admire fishers, and vice versa. This was no marketer. This was a writer.

The fishing comes before the thinking, he insisted. You may go out simply to fish with one hand and pick wild raspberries with the other, but you find yourself becoming part of the four-dimensional world of sense and spirit. You get to know the river by entering it, in the manner of Plato. You cast over wine-dark waters, and your fly falls as falls the fancy on a perfect phrase. In time you achieve the philosopher's dream—action at a distance. By then you are fishing a long line and thinking long, long thoughts.

Most of that is paraphrased from the end of Chapter XI. You will come upon more such passages throughout the text, scattered as naturally as the heartsease on a river's bank.

I have a suggestion that could help you in exploring Dr. Luce's Ireland—and may he look down to forgive me for trifling with his table of contents. He organized much of the book around the country's big, fertile loughs, reflecting the tastes of Irish and British anglers. In America, however, the lough-fishing method is today as unfamiliar as an old Celtic language. You may wish to learn it—but save it till the last.

For me, the best place to start the book is Chapter VI, on Yeats's country. Luce puts the poet in his natural setting, hiking the moors and composing verses maybe as cold and passionate as the dawn. The fishing rod becomes a passport to a tarn with dark monsters. I was shivering before I got there.

Skip then to the last chapter, which is an essay on the ethics of angling, tightly reasoned and relevant forever. I am aware of only one comparable work: *Meditations on Hunting* by José Ortega y

Gasset, who was born one year after Luce. Both were philosophers, trained to ask questions that make the rest of us squirm.

Next, try a thicker slice of the book. Take it from Chapters I, II, IV, and V—all of them on the eternal brown trout—plus III and XI on Atlantic salmon. Include the good Introduction by the author's son. In this sampler, you will find Arthur Luce as congenial a companion as Izaak Walton.

Finally, the rest of the chapters will take you to the loughs. You will be no more puzzled than I was on my first trip to Lough Sheelin. Long clinker-built boats drifted far from shore, wind amidships, each with an oarsman in the middle and anglers bow and stern. The fishermen made frequent, short casts downwind, working teams of three or four wet flies. The top droppers danced on the waves, and the big brown trout rose. Meanwhile they ignored my nymphs and streamers, which I fished deeply, scientifically.

In America, you could try the lough method on trout that are innocent of it. You would have to find a serious rowboat and transport it to a cool, fertile, breezy lake, but the trip might be worthwhile.

You will, in any case, travel in this book to an Irish countryside that is still arcadian, and you will hear an unaccustomed rhythm in the voices and the waves. You will sojourn in a place that has trout, and is therefore beautiful. You will see a grilse gleaming with the iris of the salt sea waves. Your guide will be a philosopher who loves virtue and angling.

DATUS PROPER

Bozeman, Montana
Spring, 1993

PREFACE

BOOKS on angling, other than manuals and guide-books, usually contain reflective passages, and the present work is no exception to the rule. Angling is "The Contemplative Man's Recreation", as Izaak Walton taught. The 'compleat' angler on lake or river has time for contemplation, and much to contemplate. He is in close touch with nature in her varying moods. His eyes are drawn to the horizon; and when he writes about his angling afterwards, almost inevitably he recalls the *total* experience — sights and insights, data of sense and data of spirit. Reflection is the broad, deep and quiet pool into which the stream of an angler's thought opens out from time to time.

The title of the book, *Fishing and Thinking*, draws attention to these two aspects; but the *Fishing* comes first. This is primarily a book on angling, and its *Thinking* is incidental and secondary. The *Fishing* described is angling for salmon, sea trout and brown trout on the streams and rivers, tarns and large lakes of Ireland. Most of the representative types of angling for game fish are covered, fly fishing, wet and dry, spinning, dapping and trolling; but the fly rod has pride of place. The *Thinking* ranges from angling problems proper to the weightier matters about which all men think at times. It includes studies in the causes of the 'rise' and the 'take', occasional notes on the history of places or districts where we fish, pen portraits of two gillies, notes on boatcraft, on outboard engines, on hydro-electric works as they affect the run of salmon, and on the results of official attempts to improve the angling on the western lakes.

The philosophy of the book is that of the inquiring angler, who would fain in everything 'fish and find out', who looks at life empirically and tries to see it steadily and whole. Its deeper thought is personal, but not dilettante, considered and sincere, but not professional, nor professorial.

In the final chapter the treatment is precise and studied, as is required by the ethical *motif*. Sportsmen who fish and think would not wish the ethics of their angling to be discussed and defended irresponsibly, or in ambiguous and uncertain terms. Elsewhere the argument is not obtruded or pressed. The reader who does not see eye to eye with the author on the implications of animal instinct, for instance, or on the interpretation of W. B. Yeats's poem, *The Fisherman*, should skip or skim a page or two; and he will not find, I confidently hope, his bright, beloved cast of flies here "sicklied o'er with the pale cast of thought".

I am deeply indebted to my colleague, Professor H. M. O. White, for advising on the plan of the work. I have to thank Mr. Justice T. C. Kingsmill Moore, LL.D., and Mr. E. C. Micks for reading and correcting the chapter on the Spate River. I am grateful to Mr. Erskine Childers, Minister of Lands and Fisheries, to Dr. A. J. Went of the Department of Fisheries, to the Inland Fisheries Trust, and to the Church of Ireland Printing Co., for courtesies received.

In Chapter VI, I have quoted some lines from *The Fisherman* and *The Tower*, both by W. B. Yeats. The lines are taken from these poems in *Collected Poems of W. B. Yeats*. I am much obliged to Mrs. W. B. Yeats and to Messrs. Macmillan and Co. Ltd. for kindly granting me permission to quote them.

And I cannot conclude without a brief tribute to the memory of the late Reverend Chancellor L. Parkinson Hill, who taught me to fish. He lived the good life, and he cast a lovely line.

Trinity College,
Dublin

A. A. LUCE

INTRODUCTION

A Memoir of A. A. Luce by J. V. Luce

MY Father, Arthur Aston Luce, was born and brought up in the ancient city of Gloucester. 'As sure as God's in Gloucester' was a West Country saying, and the dominating presence of the great cathedral, together with the evangelical piety of his parents, combined to impress Arthur's young mind with a strongly religious outlook. I remember his sister Dora telling me that she used to read and re-read the whole Bible two or three times a year. Arthur, too, possessed an enviable familiarity with the 'Good Book', as the many quotations in *Fishing and Thinking* testify.

His father, John James Luce, came of Jersey stock, and served for forty-six years as vicar of St Nicholas, one of the old Gloucester city churches, where a tablet is dedicated to his memory. My father recalled him as 'a man of large heart and great faith', and noted that 'the shutters were up in most of the shops in Gloucester on the day of his funeral'.

His mother was a Yorkshire woman, Alice Charles Stubbs, a cousin of Bishop Stubbs, the well-known historian. Alice was tall, fair, and constant in her devotion to her religion and her husband. On a modest income they reared a large family in the old Vicarage that went with the parish of St Nicholas. The Vicarage was a large gaunt building, which, when I last saw it, was standing forlorn and untenanted at the rear of a petrol station. In the last three decades of the Victorian era it was the brisk and cheerful home of thirteen children. Two died very young, but the rest survived to lead useful, and in some cases distinguished, lives. Cricket was a popular pastime at the Vicarage, and my father used to say that they could field a family team, a mixed 'eleven' to be sure, including five girls! The eldest boy, Frank, played for Oxford University and Gloucestershire, and went on to join the Indian Civil Service, where he rose to become District Commissioner of Bihar. Taking early retirement after the end of World War I, he had a lot to do with developing and popularising the now familiar scheme of covenanted subscriptions for the support of charities. The youngest boy, Gordon, spent much of his life as a Professor at Rangoon University, and became a world authority on the early history of Burma. Only two of the girls married: Kathleen, who became the mother of Rex Warner, the novelist; and Ethel, who graduated in medicine at Trinity College, Dublin, married an American doctor, and acquired a considerable reputation as a research dietician.

Arthur, born on 21 August 1882, was number seven in the family. Of medium height and spare build, he remained active to an advanced age, being a great devotee of a daily walk of two to three miles as the foundation of fitness. His early education was at Lindley Lodge, Nuneaton, and Eastbourne College. Like his elder brother Frank, he was a keen cricketer in his youth, and went on to become a useful opening bat for the Phoenix First XI in Dublin. As far as I know, his typically Victorian and middle-class upbringing included no acquaintance with the gentle art of angling.

Fishing, like philosophy, still lay in the future, destined to form part of the Irish experience that began with his entry to Trinity College at the turn of the century. He was following here in his father's footsteps, for the Rev. J. J. Luce was a Trinity graduate, having qualified for his BA by examinations taken as an external student. Again, like his father, Arthur too envisaged a career in the Church. After gaining his BA in 1905, he entered Trinity's Divinity School. He was duly ordained in 1907 in the Chapel of St Columba's College, securing an appointment as Chaplain to the school.

The decisive moment in his career arrived in 1912 with his election to a Trinity Fellowship on the results of a competitive examination in classics and philosophy. An attempt at Fellowship had not originally been part of his plans. He was encouraged to become a candidate by one of the Fellows, Sir Robert Tate (later to become my godfather), who had been impressed by the quality of his answers in his degree examination. While concentrating on his studies, he must also have been active in student society affairs for he was elected Auditor of the College Theological Society in 1906, delivering his inaugural address on 'The evangelical aspect of Catholic truth'. A notice of the meeting in the *Church of Ireland Gazette* concluded: 'If we mistake not, Mr Luce has a promising future before him'.

The lines of this 'promising future' were now beginning to take shape, but all hopes and plans were soon threatened with disaster in the form of the 1914–18 War. Luce enlisted in the Royal Irish Rifles, saw nearly three years active service in France, rose to the rank of Captain, and won the MC for his conduct during the battle of Passchendaele in August 1917.

Lilian Mary Thompson, a vivacious and attractive Irish girl from Granard in Co. Longford, had been one of his pre-war students in philosophy. She completed her course in 1916, obtaining first class honours and a gold medal in her final examination, and before long was working at a war-service job in Paris. The job was not without its dangers, for Paris was then under regular bombardment from the German long-range gun nicknamed 'Big Bertha'. I can still remember vividly the fear-tinged fascination with which we children used to listen to her account of how the inhabitants went about their daily work, keeping an ear cocked for the thud of the shell that landed every quarter of an hour. No doubt she thought the risk well worth it if it brought her nearer to Arthur Luce! The attachment blossomed into a formal engagement, and they were married in St Anne's Church in Dublin on 21 December 1918.

They set up house at No. 13, Bushy Park Road, Rathgar, and domestic happiness, together with good academic prospects, helped to lift the shadow of the war years. Zion Church was in full view from their front windows, and just down the road stood the rectory, where lived Arthur's piscatorial mentor, Canon Parkinson Hill. 'Zion's Hill', as he was dubbed, was a large genial man with a shock of white hair and a fine resonant voice. He could preach a good sermon, and as the *Preface* has it, 'cast a lovely line'.

Six or seven miles southwest of the city the two man-made lakes of Bohernabreena Reservoir lie in a fold of the Dublin mountains, and it was there, I think, that Canon (later Chancellor)

Hill introduced my father to the skills and pleasures of fly fishing. Bohernabreena was the scene of the incredible 'break' described in Chapter IV. In those days it was a well managed fishery with a good stock of trout. The upper and lower lakes had been formed by dams across the head-waters of the river Dodder. To us boys —John born in 1920 and Frank in 1922—it provided a playground of never-failing wonder and charm. There were trees to climb, huts to picnic in, stalactites in a cavern under the dam, and an exciting path that led round the lower lake to a primrose-filled wood. We found the boat fishing slow and boring, but the stretches of the Dodder above and below the lakes teemed with small trout, and we liked to try out our angling skills there.

Dad had taken care to initiate us young, and my first trout was taken on the fly in the Avonbeg just below the bridge at Ballinaclash. I had, I believe, just turned six, and I can still remember carrying my fingerling prize back in triumph to the car. The rivers of Co. Wicklow were great favourites with my father. He often fished the Avonmore and the Anamoe, and sometimes tried for a 'white trout' at Woodenbridge. Readers will find the lower reaches of the King's River (submerged since 1940 under Blessington lake) given star treatment in Chapter I. When that stretch was lost to him, he turned his attention to the Slaney below Baltinglass.

The 'flood' also submerged a lovely and productive stretch of the Liffey that ran from the junction with the King's River past Baltiboys Hill to the site of the dam at Poulaphouca gorge. In the Easter holidays we often motored out in our old Hillman saloon to fish in this area, and all the family were soon spread out up and down the banks casting our Garnett's Butchers and Red Spinners into every likely lie. My mother was as keen as the rest; she did not cast a long line, but she fished patiently and methodically, and once had a major triumph in taking a trout of two and a quarter pounds below Ballysmutton bridge on the upper King's River. A specimen fish for the water, it was duly stuffed and mounted, and still adorns its glass case in No. 13 (where I still live). The date was 6 May 1933.

The westward extension of my father's fishing territory came about in this way. In the spring, he used to place a 'small ad.' in the *Church of Ireland Gazette* announcing that he would be prepared to relieve a country rector of his parochial duties for the month of August, in return for the use of his rectory for a family holiday. A crucial last sentence indicated that there must be good fishing in the neighbourhood. Thus both parties secured the holiday break that they wanted, and thus it came about that after an interminable drive over dusty roads the Luce family arrived one sultry August afternoon at Tourmakeady on the western shore of Lough Mask. This was to be the setting for at least five memorable summer holidays in succession, the last two spent in the comparative luxury of Drimbawn House. We boys explored the Tourmakeady River from mouth to source, while Dad was out in the boat laying the foundations of his deep and extensive knowledge of the great lakes of Co Mayo. Here were taken the 'hundred trout, averaging two pounds in weight' (p. 109, though I believe the date was the early '30s), here many pike of 20 lb and over were landed on the troll, and from here he set out on those memorable trips to the Finney described in Chapter V.

The only thing lacking in Tourmakeady was accessible salmon and sea trout fishing. So in 1936 or 1937 my father decided to try a change of scene, moving to Ballina and the banks of the Moy where the Rectory stood just above the famous Ridge pool. Everyone approved. My mother found catering much easier, my father could catch salmon in sight of the house, and we boys were introduced to the passionate excitement of sea trout in a falling spate. The picture of the spate river in Chapter XI is a composite one built up from many happy and productive outings to the Palmerston near Killala, and the Easkey on the road to Sligo. The small mountain tarn with the large ugly trout (Chapter VI) lay high up in the Ox mountains to the south of Lough Talt. We boys found it quite a hard climb, but it was nothing to my father, who was a very fit walker and climber, and remained so well into his seventies. He used to climb Nephin every year, and last achieved this feat on his eightieth birthday.

The staple fishing in the Ballina area was provided by Lough Conn. We used to fish it out of Cloghans, being gillied first of all by Tom Timlin, and then by Michael Clark, the 'Michael' of Chapter VII. From 1941 we stayed in the hostelry run by the other family of Clarks at Cloghans. In those petrol-less days it was very convenient to be right on the lake shore. The fishing was excellent, as the table on p. 121 (based on my fishing diary) proves. There were salmon to be had in the spring, and trout all the way through from March to September. We thought the trout much freer risers than on Mask, and nearly all were taken on the wet-fly rather than dap or dry-fly. Readers will note the rise in average weight in 1943–5 combined with a falling off in numbers. We attributed this to the arrival of the tape-worm plague generated by the flooding of Blessington lake (see p.12), and the then Professor of Zoology at Trinity College, Dublin, confirmed from a specimen we provided that the trout were indeed infected in this way at the time.

My father liked the area so well that after the war he bough at bungalow on the shore of the Home Bay at Cloghans, and that was his base for spring and summer angling in the '50s and '60s. It is still in the family, owned now by my brother Frank. The lake still fishes well at times but lacks the continuous dependability of former days. 'Sally' (p.116) is now high and dry, thanks to arterial drainage which has lowered the water level by six feet or so, and the 'pool' at Brackwanshagh point (pp.125–6) is, alas, no more, but in compensation new shallows have emerged.

A survey today of the waters described in *Fishing and Thinking* does little to encourage optimism about the future of angling in Ireland. Lip service is paid to the sport's value for tourism, but more, I feel, could and should be done to protect it against the adverse factors that tend to arise from industrial and agricultural development. The summer grilse run can still give good value for money, particularly on a well-managed State fishery like the Erriff, and many lakes still hold good stocks of wild trout. But over much of the country excessive and illegal drift netting at sea, and more intensive land use, have led to a marked decline in salmon and trout returns. Pollution from pig slurry has reduced Lough Sheelin to a shadow of its once great self. Very few salmon are now taken on the Liffey, though it is perhaps remarkable that there are any at all to be had near a city that now numbers a million inhabitants. The Boyne–Blackwater system has not recovered from the combined effects of the salmon disease and a drainage scheme in the '70s. Only the lonely Dirks in their desolate corries high above Lough Mask remain much as they were fifty years ago.

But to return to A. A. Luce: I would not wish to give the impression that he did little or no work after gaining his Trinity Fellowship. On the contrary, he remained a dedicated and hard-working scholar all through his life. One does not gain a D.D. and a Litt.D., and receive an honorary doctorate from Queen's University, for nothing. The weekly visit to river or lake was the well-earned 'recreation' that literally re-created his mental zest for research and writing.

In the early '30s he hit on the vein of Berkeleian research that brought him world-wide recognition, and from then onwards article followed article and book succeeded book. He liked to rise early and work for some hours before breakfast. The loss of his wife and only daughter in a tragic accident in May 1940 might well have broken the nerve of a man of less sturdy temperament. But he faced the bereavement with stoic fortitude, pressed doggedly on with his work, and, in collaboration with his friend Dr. Jessop, brought to a successful conclusion a major re-editing of the complete works of Berkeley.

A hospitable man himself, he was helped in all this by the respect and affection of the circle of colleagues whom he met regularly on 'high table' at evening Commons. His Trinity career was a distinguished one. He held the Chair of Moral Philosophy from 1934 to 1949, when he voluntarily relinquished it to make way for a younger man. He was also Vice-Provost from 1946 to 1951. The College created a personal Chair for him in 1953, and he was active in this post for many years, teaching and publishing into his late eighties. He was the last of the Trinity Fellows to enjoy life tenure, and at his death on 28 June 1977, in his ninety-fifth year, he had been a Fellow for sixty-five years—an all-time record for the College. His portrait by Derek Hill hangs in the Common Room. Painted when he was already in his nineties, it shows the gauntness of old age, but also captures well the still keen and thoughtful gaze of the blue eyes from under the high domed forehead.

As a clergyman he never undertook parochial work, apart from the vacation duties mentioned above, but St Patrick's Cathedral claimed and received a large and willingly-given share of his time and talent. Historic links between Trinity and St Patrick's can be traced from the College's earliest days, and he was proud to continue the connection. Appointed to a Canonry in 1930, he was later promoted to become Chancellor in 1936 and Precentor in 1953. He used to point out with some glee that 'Precentor' means 'Chief Singer', whereas he could not sing a note. However, he did his duty by the Cathedral Board, duly admitted the choristers to their office, and rejoiced in the dignity and beauty of the Cathedral services. His flair for a telling and colourful phrase, and the old-world intonations of his strong clear delivery, made him a very effective preacher. On his ninetieth birthday the Cathedral bell-ringers rang a special peal to mark the occasion, and few events in his declining years gave him greater pleasure or satisfaction.

There was much deliberation over a title for this book, and I think I can claim credit for suggesting *Fishing and Thinking*. At first he was inclined to reject it, chiefly on the rather inadequate grounds that it would be jestingly changed to *Fishing and Drinking*. But in the end he accepted it as a good crisp summary of the contents. I think most readers will agree that much of the book's charm results from its unusual blend of narrative and reflection. The narrative is enriched by closely observed details of fish and fishermen in their natural surroundings. The reflections and arguments are those of a philosopher and theologian, and aim at being 'academic' in the best sense of that much-abused word (see pp. 185–6). That is to say, they aim at being clear, precise, and in touch with the realities of the situation.

Lucidity and objectivity were marked features of A. A. Luce's mind, and they were also prime characteristics of the thought and writing of his great philosophical hero George Berkeley. Luce never made any secret of the fact that he viewed the world from a Berkeleian standpoint. Much of his professional life was devoted to expounding the full and precise meaning, as he saw it, of Berkeley's philosophy. Like Berkeley, he rejected materialism, accepted the reality of the sensible world, affirmed the importance of mind as a creative and sustaining power, and believed in the existence of an eternal spirit, God, 'in whom we live and move and have our being'. This is the philosophy of 'sense and spirit' which permeates and underlies all the thought of the book. It is, I think, correct to say that the good sense and spirited quality of the work derive directly from it.

Take the observation about the foam suds on the spate river (p.151). They are really there. Both anglers see them in their true colours. But there is more to them than that. They are an intrinsic part of the whole vast meaningful world of Nature, and the anglers also see their *significance*: they are a 'sure sign that the river is falling'.

Or take the passage where Virgil is invoked to explain the 'best day on the river' (pp.36–7). Organic life and animal instinct are here finely viewed and fruitfully interpreted against the background of a spiritual universe.

Take, finally, the discussion of the ethics of angling in the last chapter. When I re-read it recently I was greatly struck by its emphatic rejection of the proposition that 'Nature is cruel' (pp.187 ff.). On the contrary, says the author, 'the course of nature is just; it may be stern but it is never cruel'. There is a sober optimism here which is morally bracing, and, I believe, spiritually profound. 'Life', he adds, 'is suffering, but life is good.' A. A. Luce lived out the truth of this striking epigram.

J. V. Luce
1990

CHAPTER I

MY BEST DAY ON THE RIVER

IN fishing you just never know. The angler must 'fish and find out', and his best fly or bait is the one that is longest on, or in, the water.

It was a hopeless-looking day in flaming June after an eight-weeks drought. No other anglers were out. I had no expectations; but fish or no fish, a day on the river is change and exercise. This unprepossessing day proved to be a day of days; it gave me the best trouting on a river I ever had. To be precise, it was the 21st day of June, 1939—the longest day in the year; it was not long enough for me, and there was no Gideon to bid the sun stand still. I wrote down the facts at the time, trying to describe the day, trying to explain it. I gave a talk about it at the time to an Anglers' Club in Dublin; but no satisfactory explanation emerged at the meeting; and now, twenty years after, I take up the record again, still wondering and trying to explain.

The scene was the King's River, a small tributary of the Liffey, some twenty miles from Dublin. The stretch I fished that day will never be fished again; it lies fathoms deep beneath the surface of the Pollaphuca reservoir. The waters were acid, and the trout, on average, small. The stretch was not preserved; the fishing was 'free'; the trout were highly educated, and knew every pattern of artificial fly served up to them. We did well, we thought, on an ordinary day if we took home half a dozen half-pounders. Most of my catch that day were about that weight; there were a few larger ones up to a pound. They were all 'nice trout', as we say; that is, well-made, firm fleshed and good eating, not the half-starved fingerlings that are taken three at a cast in some mountain tarns and Wicklow streams, soft and worthless. I kept three dozen and a half, and put back as many more. The catch was remarkable, not for the number or weight of the fish taken, but for the adverse conditions under which they were taken, and for the length of the 'rise' and the 'take'. It was almost a 'round-the clock' rise to my knowledge, and it may have been longer; it was *on* when I began, and it had not finished when I left. The weather conditions were so unpromising that no other angler came out, and I had the water to myself. I fished a fly that many anglers would think absurd. I had it on the cast; I found it worked, and I left it up. I fished from 11.30 a.m. till 10.30 p.m. with an hour off for lunch; and all that time, with scarcely any let-up, trout were rising to it and taking it. There was no noticeable hatch of fly; it was not a case of the short, sharp, mad rise, familiar to us all. For some unaccountable reason all the fish in the river were on the move all that day. I have never known anything like it. I have fished that stretch of water more times than I would wish my boss to know. I fished it spring, summer and autumn. I fished it in flood, clearing and clear. I fished it under all conditions of wind and weather, and I never met a day like that Wednesday. I returned to the same spot on the following Saturday. The conditions according to the book were better; but I could hardly stir a fin.

"Do ye know the date of the flood, Sir?" The farmer who asked me the question, like the other small-holders in the district, was a friendly man; they like to see us fishing, and often they leave their chores, and come over for a chat. The question about the flood took me aback for a moment. My thoughts flew to the Authorized Version of the Bible, and to Archbishop Ussher's* dates at the head of the columns, not put there by Ussher. But the flood in question was not Noah's Flood. It was a deluge of more immediate concern to Mick and his family; the flood to him meant notice to quit. For all that wide saucer of upland country, flanked by the Wicklow mountains, was under sentence of submersion; it was to become one of Dublin's reservoirs. All that season, as I fished, I felt in my bones its impending doom. The dam was built; the trees were felled, their branches lopped and topped; the hedgerows were cut down and burned; strong farms and humbler cottages were piles of brick and stone, rubble, cement and mortar. The district was a sorry sight, a devastated area. Any day now the flooding was due to begin, and as the waters rose inch by inch, a tiny page of human history would perish without a trace. Dublin needed the water and the power and the light; but the price of progress must be paid, and this price in anglers' eyes was high. We 'think long' for the old King's River, its winding silver stream, its gravelly banks; gone are its flowers, the pansy and bee orchis, the meadow-sweet and crow's-foot trefoil; gone are its autumn mushrooms; gone are its badger-cubs that frisked around their holes; those rich meadows where fat cattle roamed are sunless ooze and mudflats; and cannibal trouts grub in that pretty lane where my car was parked that day.

Dublin anglers will not soon forget the effect of the flooding on the fish. The story, sad enough at the time, at this distance reads like an Æsop's tale with a moral, and for prologue, my best day on the river, the 21st of June, 1939. If on that memorable day the trout were holding a carnival to celebrate their approaching liberty, things fall into place in the fable. They paid for their carnival in days to come;

*James Ussher (1581-1656), one of the first students of Trinity College, Dublin, was among the most learned men of his day. An expert in comparative chronology, he devised a scheme of time-relations to cover the events of the Biblical narrative. It is unfair to say that he dated Creation 4004 years before Christ. The formula '4004 B.C.' to any intelligent person leaves room for 4005 B.C., 4006 B.C., and an infinite series of yesterdays, sufficient to cover the astronomical figures of modern scientific speculation. Ussher is buried in Westminster Abbey.

they won their liberty from restraining banks, and liberty was their doom. When the flood came, the trout had a right royal time at first; they roamed limitless pastures, and glutted themselves with rich, unaccustomed food; in a few weeks and months those white-fleshed half-pounders became, like salmon parr in the sea, monsters; they put on weight and condition; soon they were five pounds, six pounds, seven pounds in weight, and pink as any salmon. Anglers, too, at the reservoir held high jinks, at first. Record baskets of big fish were taken. *Serva modum*; everything in moderation; nature's law was broken, and *nemesis* followed. Through their gluttony the glutted fish lost their power of resistance to disease. Next season tapeworm swept the reservoir; all the trout in it were infected, and many died; poisoning was feared, and angling was stopped for some time. The infection was carried by birds to distant waters, and even the limestone lakes of the west were, it is said, infected.

But come back now to the old King's River on that day of days. I began the day without hope because of the angling conditions. It was the tail-end of a long drought. Anticyclone seemed to have come for good and all. Fresh water, light cloud, south wind, west wind, sou'west and nor'west, hatch of fly — all these conditions favour fishing, and they were all absent that day. There had been no flood down for eight or nine weeks. The water was dead low and gin clear; every stone in the bottom was visible; in knee-waders one could cross the stream dry-foot; there was little or no fly on the water, nothing that could be called a hatch. The June sun flamed down all day, practically without a cloud. The wind was nor'east, and remained in that airt* all day; the only redeeming features of the weather were that the wind was steady and upstream.

No one could have known in advance of experience what that day had in store for the angler. Fishing and thinking are alike in that respect; you get nowhere in advance of experience. The angler must fish and find out; the thinker

* i.e., quarter.

must try out his theories in practice, and he gets nowhere by abstract *a priori* reasoning. The laws of fishing, like the so-called laws of thought and laws of nature, are useful generalizations from experience, but no more; they indicate what generally does happen but not what must happen. In trying to understand the behaviour of trout, as in trying to grasp the nature of truth, this attitude, technically called *empirical*, is essential. There are no 'causes' of the behaviour of trout, if by 'cause' we mean a mechanical force acting on an animated machine, and mechanically producing effects. Wind and weather and temperature are not 'causes' in any such sense; they do not initiate or compel the movements of trout; they are not active causes; they are simply passive conditions under which the fish rise or go down, take the lure or refuse it, follow it or come short at it. The experienced angler can read these conditions, as we read writing and other signs; he can usually form a shrewd opinion as to his chances; but he is often wrong; and there is only one way of finding out whether it is a good fishing day or not; and that is to fish and find out. Experience is the only test.

I drove my small car down the boreen,* and parked it literally at the water's edge, within a few yards of the stepping-stones. In low water the lads and lassies hopped nimbly across from stone to stone, while the sedate cart, drawn by horse or ass, ferrying the seniors, splashed through the sand and gravel of the adjacent ford. I put up my rod, fitted the reel, greased the line, attached the cast, oiled the fly and began operations at the little run below the stepping-stones, where every angler wets his cast, and where the trout know every pattern of fly from A to Z. As soon as the fly touched the water, a half-pounder rose and took it, took well. As soon as he was in the bag, came another surprise; a big fish swirled, came with a head and tail rise, took and broke me. Then I knew there was something up; for the larger fish, a pound and over, hardly ever rise in daytime on the King's River; that is why they are large fish. Apologies for the break; the cast and its fly were

* *Anglice*, lane.

left over from a previous evening, and had been worked hard then. In dry-fly work on these small mountainy streams one fishes more or less continuously, the gut or nylon gets drawn, and if one meets the monarch of the pool, a break may occur.

And now a word on casting-method. Waters differ and anglers differ. The method that suits one stream or one man will not suit another stream or another man. Here on these upland streams there is little fly as a rule; one may look all day and not see the tell-tale circle of the rising fish. In such waters self-limitation to 'fishing the rise' is out of the question, at any rate to a young and active angler. The 'minor tactics' of a chalk stream become the major strategy of the King's River, and similar streams. The method that suited the King's River, as I knew it, might be called 'fishing the spot', and it was the method I used that day. Guided ever by experience, select your likely spot and put your fly on it. The purist, self-limited to 'fishing the rise', might dub the method 'chuck it and chance it'; but that label, which does not fitly describe even wet-fly work, *a fortiori* is quite inappropriate to the dry-fly work of 'fishing the spot'. All casting is 'chancing' to some extent; but good casting is certainly not 'chucking'. There is casting and casting; just as there is purism and purism. Purism in angling as in other occupations is an ambiguous term. The purism that strives after artistic excellence is much to be desired; the purism that frowns on the lawful methods employed by other folk is narrow and narrowing. The power to vary one's method with the situation is the mark of the expert, and is far superior to concentration on one method. Fish the rise, if you see it, of course; but what is the angler to do if he sees no rise? Sit down and wait? That is 'lazy man's waiting'; he might be sitting and waiting all day, and see no rise. If the trout are not rising, and the angler has the knowledge and skill to make them rise, he is an artist with the right to practise his art. There is no point of principle involved. 'Fishing the rise' is not intrinsically superior to other casting-methods; it is not even more 'sporting'. There is no essential difference between a trout 'on the rise', and any other trout; if not actually rising, he is often poised, ready to rise; and the angler who can touch off the rise deserves his success.

'Fishing the spot' in some waters is a finer art than 'fishing the rise', more exacting and more sporting. It is discriminating and carefully aimed, and is not just throwing at the water in general. It calls for exact knowledge of the spot to fish, when the fish does not tell you where. Any novice can rise a hungry rising trout who gives his haunt away; but to stir a fat, old, indolent fish lying out of sight deep down by that clump of weeds — that task will tax your powers. The angler who fishes the spot must know the spot to fish; he must know where the trout lie, or are likely to lie, and must place his fly accordingly. Knowledge, skill and perseverance are required; the habits of trout vary from river to river, from day to day; they vary with the height of the water; they vary with the strength and direction of the wind; they vary with the season of the year and even with the time of day.

Far from 'chucking and chancing', the angler is cleverly placing his fly where he wants to place it; he is casting cunningly a small, light, feathery object at a small spot. He must place his fly *con amore*, tenderly, precisely, thus, there. His rod and line and cast must be, as it were, extensions of his arm and hand and finger. There! There! See his fly alight, soft as sleep, in the swirl at the head of the run. It is well cocked up. Follow it. See. It floats gaily, deftly guided, down the narrow channel between that humpy sandbank and the patch of swaying weeds. That is where I would choose to feed, "if I were a trout, swimming about". " 'Tis not in mortals to command success." The angler deserves it, who can place his fly there, thus.

'Fishing the spot' was the method used on the day in question, and it was justified by its results. Natural rises were few and far between. 'Fishing the rise' would have meant indolence, unproductive indolence. There was no water for the wet fly. Dry-fly fishing the spot suited the situation well. For the greater part of that day I was rising trout every five or ten minutes.

Replacing the lost fly with another of the same pattern, I worked upstream from the stepping-stones for a mile or so, enjoying the fishing, and the liberty, and the variety of the stretch. The King's River here is, or rather was, a one-bank river (if the expression may pass). The current swings east and west, alternately, in reaches some fifty yards, or more, in length, leaving on one side a shelving slope of sand and gravel, hardly to be called a 'bank', on which you stand and cast, and on the other side a steepish, under-cut bank, ten or twenty feet high, towards which you look and cast. One could cast from either side, of course, and catch fish; but to fish from the shelving slope was usually more convenient; it saved one the bother of carrying a net. A net is not needed, unless you are fishing from the high bank. On the other side the shelving slope serves the purpose of the net. If you hook your trout from there, you need no net; the slope is sufficient. You shall not try to 'yank him out', of course; you shall treat your fish with respect, or he may not remain 'yours'. Take his measure; judge his size and weight, as soon as you can; treat him sternly, but not rudely or roughly; draw him at once, if you can, away from his holt in the bank; steer him clear of the tangling weeds, where his safety lies; he will try to keep in the full current; but as he weakens, edge him towards the shelving sand and gravel at your feet; as he comes towards you, step back, like a shy partner at a dance, keeping out of sight; for "the fear of you and the dread of you" are upon the fish, as well as on bird and beast, as God promised Noah.* Every trout we grass illustrates that truth. So keep out of sight as long as you can, if you want to land your fish; it is a useful maxim for fishers and others. In playing your fish, feel him firmly all the while. If he wants line, let him have it; but give him no slack. Wait for the pause in his struggles, and when he is quiet, ease him little by little out of the current into the still water, and thence into the

* Genesis ix, 2.

shallows; and so, watching your chance, slide and glide him over the pebbles, until he is high and dry.

In this way I took a dozen or so good trout before lunch, besides the pinkeens I put back. Returning to my car, well satisfied with the morning's work, I made myself a cup of tea, took a short *siesta* and prepared to resume the struggle.

The rest of the day followed the pattern of the morning, and I tell its story in brief, leaving the explanation attempted for Chapter II. A good morning on the King's River, as on other waters, was usually followed by a poor afternoon, and I expected little when I took up the rod again. I walked half a mile downstream, and set to work half-heartedly, like a lotus-eater in the land where "'tis always afternoon". The sun shone from a cloudless sky pitilessly; the air was heavy with midsummer, midday heat; the breeze was still nor'east; but I continued casting, and the trout continued to respond. They must have gone quiet for a while, I think; for my record shows that I changed the fly, and put up the Wexford Governor; but after killing one fish on it I returned to my first love, and used it for the rest of the day. The basket on my back grew heavier, and my heart grew proportionately lighter.

The heat of the day was now over. The cattle left the water's edge, and began to roam the pastures. Rabbits came out from their stifling burrows to drink and graze. Shadows lengthened. My shadow fell across the stream, and I had to stand well back, and cast a long line. White moth came out; several trouts rose to them, and some fell to my white-winged fly. A bat fluttered by, and made an offer at it. That was the signal. It is time to quit. Working back to the stepping-stones where my day began, I took another fish from that pool, and rose the big fellow, I believe, that broke me eleven hours previously. Then I knocked off, reeled up, and took down the rod. The rise was not over; but honour was satisfied. My best day on the river was finished. A twenty-mile drive lay before me, and I must not keep the household up.

CHAPTER II

THE WHY AND THE WHEREFORE

A REMARKABLE day's trouting was described in the previous chapter. Can it be explained? To try to explain it and determine its why and its wherefore are the tasks of this chapter. Why did well-educated trout on a well-fished stream on Wednesday the 21st day of June, 1939, in bright sunshine and a nor'east breeze, rise freely all day to an artificial fly, known as the Coachman and usually regarded as an evening fly,* and take it with rare avidity. The question looks well beyond one particular day and its personal interest; and the answer touches on the why and the wherefore of angling experiences that all anglers meet on their best days and their worst. For one cannot hope to understand and explain the particular experience of a special day without a good deal of general knowledge about the way of a trout with a fly.

Why do trout ever swallow artificial flies? We take their habit for granted, and are rather prone to assume that they ought to swallow what we offer, and are full of excuses for them and ourselves when they do not do so. It was too hot, too cold, too bright, too dark; there was no breeze;

* The Coachman is a useful general purposes fly for the evening of life, too. When sight grows too dim to follow other flies, the Coachman can still be seen.

it was blowing a gale; there was no fly on the water; there was too much fly, and the fish were glutted. Before we look for reasons why they do *not* take, we ought to spend a little thought on the previous question; we ought, in fact, to ask, Why do fish ever take our flies?

A bunch of feathers and a steel hook — what is the attraction there? The broad answer in the case of trout, not salmon, is imitation. The artificial fly must imitate the natural fly. The imitation need not be close or particular. Exact copying is unnecessary, often impossible, and it may defeat its own end; but in general our fly must look good to eat, and must behave in the water like something the trout know to be good to eat, or they will not be convinced, or even interested.

Fly-tying is a fine art, giving scope to angling imagination; but, as Lord Bacon said of something else, it is "no match for the subtlety of nature".* We may copy the fly in repose; but if it has not life and movement, in the water it will not deceive. And what right have we to expect a clever trout to be deceived? Trout must eat to live. That principle cuts both ways; it means that the trout must sometimes take a chance; but it also means that he spends much of his time in discriminating between what is good to eat, and what is not, as his forbears have done since the evolutionary Year One. Nature has endowed trout with powers of discrimination of a high order. They have amazing sight for colour and shades of colour, for shape, size and motion; they appear to have a sense of smell, and if they do not hear, as some say, they certainly have a keen sense of auditory vibrations. Izaak Walton made as little noise as he could when he was fishing, he says; and he advises anglers "to be patient, and forbear swearing, lest they be heard, and catch no fish".†

Here is a typical felicity, worth a moment's pause, of Izaak's thought and style. At first sight the words quoted look like a trite moral sentiment, arising out of a rather heavy discussion as to whether fish can hear. Dwell on the

* *Novum Organum,* I, xiii. † *The Compleat Angler,* I, v.

words, and you catch their overtones and undertones. "... lest they be heard" — in those simple words the artist blends his humorous suggestion that the trout overhear the swearing, and refuse to come and be caught, with the not-uncommon belief that angling success and failure have some connection with the appointed sanctions of virtue and vice!

The trout's powers of inhibition are amazingly efficient; he dashes to take, and at 'the fishological moment' (as a gillie once said), he checks, like an instantaneous self-acting brake. With an upward spring and a leap, head and tail out of the water, he strikes at the bait, touches it perhaps, but does not take. You can see the check sometimes when the water is clear, with the slope sun behind the drifting boat, especially if you are wearing polarized sun-glasses. What is that in the water beside my fly? A rock? No, it is a big brown trout; and he is gone, as instantaneously as he appeared. Dapping on Lough Mask in Monastery Bay near the Irish College, I once saw the process to perfection and to my full satisfaction. I was dapping with a grasshopper and two daddies, a very conspicuous bait. Suddenly he appeared from nowhere, and circled the bait; he studied the mixed grill from every angle, and was satisfied. He came; he checked; he was conquered.

For their further protection trout have the half-take, usually called 'coming-short'. Anglers dislike this habit intensely, and are often unrighteously indignant about it; we regard the trout's coming-short as a very definite short-coming in the species. On reflection in a cool hour we can, however, hardly help seeing it as a wonderful piece of instinctive behaviour, a provision of nature to ensure the survival of this game fish. Salmon and trout come-short when they are interested in the fly, but not convinced. Pinkeens practise it; as soon as your fly meets the water, there is a splash and a splutter and a tiny tug, and he is off; he has come-short. The big trout do it, when the clouds are gathering, and the wind rising, and there's 'a drop in the mouth of the wind'. They do it, too, in fine and settled weather. Counter-measures, such as shortening line or changing fly, sometimes succeed, but not often. Usually there is nothing to be done, but smile and bear it. It is certainly no good blaming oneself or being down on one's luck; it is far better to praise the fish, and put up with it, as one puts up with 'pretty Fanny's little ways'. Half a dozen varieties of coming-short can be distinguished. There are: (1) the rise and the 'boil', but no touch, (2) the follow-up, often to within a yard of the boat, and then the 'boil' as he goes down, (3) the under-water pull without anything to see; sometimes it is a mere check, hardly detectible; sometimes it is a chuck, and sometimes a smart pull that takes a turn or two out of the reel; the under-water pull is almost always to the tail-fly, for the obvious reason that it is lowest in the water. The commonest type is (4) the tweak, usually to the bob-fly; this fine piece of gymnastic on the trout's part is most annoying at the other end of the rod and line, like a runaway knock; the angler sees and feels the fish, and feels, rightly or wrongly, that if he had been a bit quicker on the strike, he would have hooked the fish. On the 'foul-hook' see below (p. 23); I doubt whether it should be classed with coming-short; but I ought to mention (5) a nondescript type of mis-hooking; it occurs before rain, and is perhaps the supreme test of patience and self-command; for he takes out line, gives you play, and you feel he is yours, but he is not. You hook him, hit him hard, and you feel he is well on; and he seems so in front of the drifting boat; but as soon as you swing him to the back, and the pull comes from a different direction, the hold is released, and your fly comes back to a sadder and no wiser man. When it happens time after time, take a chance, and try to net in front of the boat.

When trout come-short, what exactly are they doing? In some of the cases, listed above, they are clearly not feeding, but simply playing with the fly; they are up near the surface, perhaps for warmth, interested in the weather and what is going on, but not interested in food. In other cases they are feeding selectively; they are 'choosey'; they are disposed to feed, but more from habit than from hunger;

they do not gulp down your fly with an honest mouthful of water; but instead they nip a wing or hackle without touching the hook. The precision of sight involved and the precision of movement seem to us miraculous. Trout come-short in a high wave as easily as in a flat calm; they come-short at flies drawn rapidly through the water; they come-short at trolled spoons and devons bristling with hooks; they come-short — and this, perhaps, is the greatest miracle of all — at natural baits which they certainly recognize as good to eat. They come-short at dapped mayfly in the mayfly season, or at the dapped daddy. Place two daddies on your hook; one will be taken, the other left. When this has happened two or three times in five minutes the dapper will need all his patience and good temper; he will be bombarded with advice from the other occupants of the boat. "Give him time." "No, strike at once." "Hit or miss." "Count ten from the rise." "No, count three."

The trout's greatest accomplishment in this line, displaying an almost perfect command of appetite and desire, is his power of coming-short at the solid natural bait, say the grasshopper garnished with one or two daddy-long-legs. There it is bobbing up and down attractively in a smart breeze, the sun lighting up the glinting green and red of the hopper and the grey gauze of the daddy's wing. See. It has gone down. He's got it. Steady now. Count ten, as Michael bids, or you will pull it out of his mouth. One, two, three, four . . . surely he has it now, and it has him; for the floss silk is moving slowly away. Five, six, seven, eight . . . the ten moments are ten eternities; but they pass. Strike now, says Michael, and you strike. And the dap comes back to you, minus a hopper's leg.

Part of the explanation is that it is not altogether a question of appetite. Habit has much to say to it. The sated trout comes to the bait out of habit, just as the lusty salmon, fresh up from the sea, twenty pounds in weight, without need for food or desire for it, on a summer evening in his native river, lunges at spinners and microscopic midge, as he did when a fingerling parr. It is not appetite, but force of habit. The instinct of play may be there in a rudimentary form. Trout seem to do things for fun at times, as if they enjoyed taking a rise out of the angler. They have anger in their composition, too. A salmon will chase an intruder from his pool, and a red prawn sets him wild. Trout show annoyance, too; they jump on the bait, as if to drown it; or they lash with tail or fin, and often get 'foul-hooked' for their pains; he has refused to take the hook, and the hook takes him.

A trout weighing three or four pounds, reared in a limestone lake, must certainly be four or five years old; reared in acid water, he is probably a good deal older. What practice in selection he has had! Half a dozen times a day for six or seven months a year he sees artificial flies, baits and other dangerous lures. In running water, small brooks and streams, where bottom feeding is not plentiful, your trout is more dependent on food moving swiftly by, and he must take greater risks. Yet in spite of the daily and hourly dangers many trout survive to a considerable age. Nature has prepared them well for their task of living dangerously, and has taught them to be careful what food they take, and when, and how. The resources, outlined above, are at their command. The wonder is that we ever catch any of them at all. Their native tendency to check and look before they leap has issued in schooled and practised inhibitions. Self-restraint has become their second nature; their discrimination would do credit to a diplomat.

Such considerations enter into and govern the explanation of any 'take'; it may be an exceptional and long-continued take such as the one described above, or the ordinary, all-too-brief take which anglers meet every day, or hope to meet; in either case we are trying to determine the reasons for the weakening or suspension of the trout's protective inhibitions. In a problem of this sort there are no positive, real, causing causes; there are no magical powers in the artificial fly; no angel descends and troubles the pool. When we seek to explain and find the cause or causes of a piscatorial phenomenon, such as a rise or take, we are looking for the condition, or conditions, under which the trout's normal caution is relaxed, his inhibitions are weakened, and his niggling nibble is transformed into a bold gulp.

The main conditions affecting the trout's actions and reactions are three in number: (1) the trout's appetite and the food supply, (2) the wind, and (3) the weather. These three sets of conditions are familiar to all anglers, and are accepted by all as explanations. I shall say something about each set, both in general and with particular reference to 21 June, 1939; but I do not believe that the behaviour of the fish that day can be explained solely in terms of the three sets of conditions mentioned above. I shall therefore suggest a fourth condition, and submit it with some trepidation to the reader's judgment. It is not generally accepted, and I am not as clear about it myself as I would wish to be; but one often finds in life that the deepest reasons are not the clearest; they are so close to us, so *intime*, that we cannot set them at arm's length and see them in perspective. For want of a better name let me call the fourth condition 'psychological'; and I will explain what I mean when I come to it.

First, about the trout's food and feeding habits in so far as they affect angling. A hungry trout, other things being equal, will be quicker off the mark, and sooner on the prey; his inhibitions are weakened by his hunger, and he is so much the easier to catch. Trout well mended after spawning are hungry; in lakes they take the trolled bait freely in March; but gradually go off it in May and June. Trout, gashed by pike, or otherwise injured, and on the mend are hungry and will take fly or bait when other trout will not. Sated trout rarely take. On a warm July afternoon, when the sun is behind the boat, you may see great plump trouts, swimming lazily after your team of flies with the dignity, deportment and detachment of aldermen fed on turtle soup. The wholesale removal of perch and eels from the big lakes benefits the trout; does it improve the trout angling? Those who have watched both processes on the spot are very doubtful as to the answer to the question.

More food for the trout does not mean more trout for the angler; it may mean less; for when there is much bottom feeding and few competitors for it, the trout become bottom-feeders, and no longer rise freely and hungrily to the fly.

Trout would seem to have their meal-hours; but they do not keep regularly to their timetable. Most anglers agree that some hours of the day are better for their purpose, and some hours worse. On the large lakes of the west of Ireland few anglers fish before 10 a.m., and that not alone for their own convenience, but because the trout are not early risers. Normally one does not get a rise before 11 a.m., and then it is just a solitary outpost or scout or sentry; and he does not mean business as a rule. Between noon and 1.30 p.m. the lake wakes up; 'rises' and 'takes' are often frequent. From 2 p.m. to 3.30 p.m. is generally a slack period, especially on a warm and sunny day. One looks for a four o'clock rise, and from that hour on can be a very responsive and productive period. If the evening is warm, and the breeze holds, the larger trout will take till sundown, and one four-pounder will redeem a blank day. Most gillies will gladly stay out as long as there is a chance of a fish; those who tell the visitor that trout never take after 6 p.m. are under orders from the guest-house to have you back for dinner at 7 p.m., or maybe there's a bit of hay wants saving. Both are good reasons for reeling-up.

The foregoing sketch of a timetable has a basis in experience, and it helps the angler to plan his own meal-hours; it certainly applies to some rivers and lakes; but what it means in terms of the trout's feeding habits is not easy to say. Do they surface when they are feeding, or when they are not feeding? When the long hours pass without a pull, are the trout lying 'doggo' under a rock, dreaming of next year's mayfly season, or are they voraciously pursuing minnows and perch-fry, or grubbing up water-snails and the slimy things that haunt the shores. In any case any trout-timetable only holds in a general way, and is liable to be torn to tatters by exceptional events. The trout world, like the Church, has its movable feasts; on such occasions anything may happen.

The greed of fish is proverbial, and trout in this respect are no better than they should be. In the mayfly season, their dietary knows neither hour, law nor limit; they gorge on the greenfly, and when the blackfly first comes out, they gorge on it. The hatch of fly on the Westmeath lakes must be seen to be believed.* I have seen the surface of Lough Sheelin so plastered with green drake, that one could hardly find a spot to place one's dap, and at midnight there, when it was too dark to see, I have heard the 'suck, suck, suck' of the great trouts leisurely cruising round the boat, and swallowing their fill of the spent gnat. A spate in a river has a similar effect; a gorge on worms is followed by a glut; the trout are distent with food, and will not look at bait or fly for days afterwards.

One would like to know what part the natural fly plays in the normal diet of the average trout. Does its presence or absence make much difference to the trout? Fly on the water, even midge and inconspicuous fly which the trout are not taking, seems to keep them moving and alert, and therefore more ready to take the artificial. It makes a difference to the angler; but to the big trout of the lakes the ordinary small flies, other than the mayfly, can hardly be much more than an appetizer or *bonne bouche*. Where the fish are fat and firm-fleshed, there is almost always plenty of bottom feeding, such as water-snails, etc.; in many waters, both running water and still water, there are reeds and rushes thickly covered with grubs and suchlike evil beasts, which the trout enjoy. It is a point of some importance to the angler; for if the natural fly as food means comparatively little to the trout, we cannot expect him to be deeply interested in our artificial flies. That he is interested in them at times makes one think that our flies appeal to something more than appetite; the trout may take them from curiosity, from surprise; and perhaps even from anger, dislike and fear. Certainly the trout that took my Coachman on the day in question were not hungry trout, as I show below. Hunger was not the explanation.

* See below (p. 139).

Turn now to the wind and weather, and let us discuss their effect on angling. The wind, its direction, strength, degree of steadiness and temperature have much to say to the rise of trout and the take. It is one of the first lessons the young angler learns. Your boat is becalmed. Cast with the finest of nylon and the smallest of flies, and there is no response. A ruffle of wind comes, and at once you are into a trout. Why is this? It is partly due to the physical properties of the wind; the air in motion stirs the surface of the water, disposes the trout to come to the surface, and at the same time stirs the fibres of the fly, and makes it more attractive and more deceptive.

The quality of the wind is of great importance, too, and this is determined largely by its direction. Everyone knows the lines, or some variety of them, which are given in Bentham's *Book of Quotations* in the following form:

When the wind is in the east,
It's neither good for man, nor beast.

When the wind's in the south,
It blows the bait to the fishes' mouth.*

When the wind's in the west,
The weather is at the best.

And for the benefit of anglers someone has added:

When the wind is from the north,
Seldom the angler ventures forth.

The lines contain truth; but the following modifications and qualifications are necessary. The south wind favours angling, if it is dry and warm and blowing softly, like St. Paul's south wind;† but there is a cold, wet, gusty south, the precursor of rain and gale, that sends every trout to the bottom. The east wind is almost always bad; it has a tang and a sting, and is generally gusty, and fish hate the feel of

* *The Compleat Angler*, I, v:
. . . when the wind is South
It blows your bait into a fish's mouth.

† "When the south wind blew softly", Acts xxvii, 13.

it on their nebs; but they will take in it sometimes, if there is a good hatch of fly. The west wind in the west of Ireland is not popular with all anglers; it is either strong or unsteady. The 'westerly air-stream', as the forecasts term it, is almost always too strong, and on the large lakes it produces those deep-down agitations or undulations which the gillies call 'the working* of the lake', and which persist after the wind has died down. Trout rarely take when the lake is 'working'. The westerly air-stream is often cold. The mild west wind is fluky and unsteady, swinging to and fro between nor'west and sou'west. There is a bitter north wind which chills the angler and kills the hatch of fly and the rise of trout; but there is also a cool and steady north wind, which drives away the steamy mists and fogs, gives clear and sparkling air, puts the big trout in good heart, and makes them come at the fly with 'attack'.

On the intermediate points of the compass it is hard to generalize. On the whole the nor'west wind is best, but it is apt to rise and become a gale. A steady, dry sou'west is good; but when it backs and rises, there will be rain, and the trout will go down and stay down. In a mild and steady sou'east you may fish in hope. The nor'east wind is a problem; there are two nor'easters: the one blusters, the other kisses. The former is strong and bitterly cold; it may

> Hunger into madness
> Every plunging pike;†

but it sends trout to the bottom; and it should send wise anglers home to a hot bath and bed. The other nor'easter one does not often meet; but when it comes, it is good, and is good for fishing; it is a breeze, rather than a wind; it clears the air, and when the day warms up, it puts an edge on the trout's appetite. It blew all day on 21 June, 1939. Before I wet a line that morning, I mounted one of the stepping-stones, I remember, to look around and take stock of the day. I turned my cheek to the breeze, and sensed a special quality

* Cf. "The sea wrought and was tempestuous", Jonah i, 11.
† Charles Kingsley, *Ode to the North-East Wind.*

in it; and I said to myself, "There is something in that breeze, a *je ne sais quoi*, a warmth, a coolness and a caress." The air seemed electric and alive, and for the joy of living in this good world, like the Psalmist, "I opened my mouth, and drew in my breath",* and thought of the Infinite.

A warm and steady breeze is always an asset. Rough, gusty and strong winds are always bad. A flat calm on the lake is almost always useless; but there are exceptions to every rule in fishing. A warm breeze (other things being equal) is better than a cold breeze; but in estimating temperature for angling purposes, the ratio of air to water must always be borne in mind; and some anglers carry thermometers for the purpose.

Wind and weather conditions are all relative to their background and context, and their effect on the behaviour of fish may vary accordingly. For instance, a nor'west wind *after a north wind* is almost always good; *after a west wind* it is not so good. A sou'east wind *after an east wind* may give you trout; but a similar sou'east wind *that has backed from south* would not be so favourable. The moisture-content of the wind affects the trout strongly; they do not like misty, smoky or humid air, any more than we do; heavy hanging cloud masses depress them; they like dry clear air, with sunshine, not too prolonged, and light clouds, well broken up.

Finally, the angler must remember that change in itself is good, where trout are sullen. A cloud on a sunny day may bring them up; a gleam of sun on a dull day may give you a fish. Rain after a dry spell, or a clearance after rain may work the oracle. "Any change," said Michael one day when we had been flogging the lake hour after hour without response, "any change in the weather would be an improvement, even a change for the worse." It is a perfect Bull — a truth in a jest.

Rain has a great effect on the feelings and movements of trout. Rain in prospect is one thing; rain falling is another thing; and fresh water in river or lake is different again. Rain threatening almost always puts the trout down,

* Psalm cxix, 131 (P.B.V.).

especially if the temperature falls. When rain *begins* to fall there is always a chance of a fish, and the first few drops of warm rain, when swallows are flying low and picking fly off the surface, are sometimes charged with magic. A showery day often means a good basket. Long-continued rain puts trout down; cold, driving rain puts an end to fishing.

Now comes the hardest part of my task. I have to state a case for a psychological factor, or something like it, in the conditions of the take. It is not a mystical factor; the case is based on angling experience. It is not a religious factor necessarily, though it disposes of the case for irreligion and materialism. But it is a factor that transcends our workaday categories of mechanical explanation. Every angler of experience meets strange happenings, such as the rise and take, described in the previous chapter. Such happenings are of a piece with happenings in a much wider sphere; and they remain unexplained and inexplicable unless we assume that there are more things in heaven and earth than materialism can explain or even recognize. The psychological factor requires the thoughtful angler to assume a spiritual basis for life and existence. If trout and other living things are regarded as machines that react mechanically to external stimuli, their behaviour in general, and in particular their exceptional mass movements and impulses, are inexplicable.

In calling this factor 'psychological' we do not credit fish with possessing a 'psyche' or mind, like the human mind. Trout do not look before and after; they do not expect and remember, as we do; they have little or no centre of individuality; they have no responsibility. Still they are not machines; they feel pain and pleasure; they partake in the world soul or life, and that was the original meaning of the Greek word *psyche*; hence this aspect of their behaviour may be called, and is, psychological. *Sociological* would be a better term in some respects; for fish live largely in their *societas* or species or community; but 'sociology' has become identified in the public mind with the study of human society; and therefore the broader term 'psychological factor', in its original Greek sense, is to be preferred.

The ancient Greeks were firmly convinced that there was a bond of sympathy between all living things. Some of their philosophers maintained that the world itself was alive. "All things share the breath of life," said one of them. Without some such principle which we may call *the principle of psychological sympathy* it is impossible to give a rational account of the mass movements of fish and other living things. Two anglers are comparing notes on a day's fishing; one has fished the north end of the lake, the other the south end, and twenty miles of water lay between them. "What time did the trout come on, Tom?" "There was a short rise at 11, and a longer rise at 5.30, William." "That is curious, Tom; it was exactly the same with us." Curious or not curious, that experience is a commonplace with anglers; and we are inclined to pass it over lightly with the observation, "Oh, yes; the same causes produce the same effect." But we are not doing full justice to the facts, unless we include 'psychological sympathy' among the 'same causes'. The individualism that dominates our workaday thinking about ourselves and our environment breaks down in all such cases. Individualism is not the whole truth, or the sole truth about the individual; nor is socialism the whole truth, or the sole truth, about society. Man is a social individual; and there is a bond of sympathy between socialized or socializing individuals, that extends beyond the species *man*, and to a degree is found universally.

Michael has watched the ways of trout at close quarters for over half a century. He is a shrewd observer, and he says that a yawning angler rarely gets a trout; he means that if the angler is sleepy, probably the fish are sleepy, too. Conditions, within limits, that get us down, put them down. Conditions that cheer us, cheer them. If the angler feels 'nesh', as folk in Gloucestershire say, the fish feel 'nesh', too; if the angler is 'sprack', the fish will be 'sprack', too. All things 'conspire'; they share the breath of life.

When the cattle are lying down at the water's edge, or

standing in the shallows with drooped heads, flicking the flies away with lazy tail, as if no blade of grass was left, when the raucous seagulls are silent and still, or preening their feathers on rock and stone, when there is not a swallow to be seen, and the air is thick and humid, and Mount Nephin is wrapped in cloud, and there is a halo round the milky sun, and white wisps of fog rise from the water-meadows, accept the verdict, tireless angler. Give it up for the time being; acquiesce in the general feeling; put down the rod; go ashore, and have a cup of tea; for under those conditions not even the apostle's 'south wind blowing softly' could give you a trout.

But see, a change is coming. Michael is staring at the mountain; yes, the cloud is lifting; a shift of wind has scattered the mist, and cleared the air, and whipped up the dancing waves, and melted their leaden hue. The cattle have left the shore, and are munching in the pastures; the swallows are chivying the flies, and the gulls and shapely terns are scouting far and wide. Into your boat, angler; out on the drift, and do not strike too hard!

The fellow-feeling in nature, the natural sympathy between kind and kind, is raised to a higher power and reaches its climax in the mass movements of individuals within the kind or species. The flighting of duck at dusk and dawn, the wheeling squadrons of golden plover in a high wind, the evening exercises of rooks and starlings, the mad, purposeful dance of a myriad spinners on a summer's evening, the buzzing beehive and teeming ant-hill — these familiar wonders show that individual living organisms are not imitative machines, but are instinct with some family life and family feeling of a semi-spiritual character that must at times be taken into account; and if we call it the 'psychological factor', we shall not be far wrong; for it is a phase of the Life Force, the *élan vital*, or World Soul, and ultimately, for Christians and other theists, it is the gift of the Universal Spirit in whom we live and move, have our being* and do our thinking.

* Acts xvii, 28.

Aaron's rod budded. An account of an exceptional fishing day on the King's River has blossomed out into an outline sketch of a philosophy of life. We are trying to explain the fact that on the 21st day of June, 1939, under angling conditions for the most part adverse, educated trout, usually stiff and cautious, on a public stretch of water rose freely to an artificial fly, named the Coachman, an evening fly with white wing and peacock body, and took it greedily in the morning, at midday, in the afternoon, in the evening, at dusk and to the edge of dark.

Hunger was not the cause. The normal food supply of the King's River was quite adequate; the trout taken that day were well-nourished; they were in fact as fat as butter. Two whole minnows dropped from the mouth of one of them; there were plenty of minnows shoaling in the shallows; the stones had their water-snails and the reeds their usual complement of grubs and slugs. Abundance of bottom-feeding was available. It was not hunger that made the trout take the fly that day.

Nor was it the state of the water. No fresh water of any considerable volume had been down for eight or nine weeks, and the water was low, relatively stale and gin clear. Flood water is said to oxygenate the water, and put heart and attack into the trout's movements; and one often finds it so on the Wicklow streams. Three or four days after a flood, when the trout have worked off the effects of their gorge on worms, they come on the fly greedily for an hour or so; but in this case there had been no flood down, no gorge on worms, and yet the take continued for the livelong day. On the state of the water the trout should have been lethargic and cautious; in fact they were full of dash and attack; they leaped before they looked.

If the cause was not in the trout's tummies, or in their habitat, what about the ceiling of their dwelling-space, the air and upper air, the wind and weather? Their ceiling that day was warm to hot, and bright to glaring. Midsummer sunshine, midsummer heat, and nor'east wind — would any experienced angler expect those conditions to yield their best day on the river? I think not. In weighing the net effects of these conditions, we must take them together, not separately. The long sunshine, the heat and the nor'east wind, taken separately, would tell against good fishing; they form a trio of adverse conditions; yet taken together they may have formed a group, not unfavourable. Philosophers speak of the 'composition of causes'; and here certainly we must take the weather conditions 'in composition'. Trouts' eyes are sensitive to bright light; and long-continued sunshine, especially with the vertical rays of summer, tends to put them down. Summer heat, especially the sultry heat of a cloudless summer's afternoon, has the same effect. And a touch of east in the wind, as a rule, is a drawback.* Now 'compound' these conditions, as the chemist 'compounds' the bitter and the sweet. Think of them together. Put the June sun with its flaming light and scorching heat along with the keen, cool nor'east breeze. How would they *together* affect the trout? The glaring sun on high, shining straight down into his sensitive eyes would tend to put him down, and so would the keen air, stinging his neb. Taken together those unpleasant effects might cancel out. Taken together the combination of conditions might even encourage him to rise. That summer's day was what is called in Ireland 'a pet day', nature's unexpected *largesse*. And part of my theory (but only a part) is that the nor'east wind pleasantly cooled the surface water, neutralized the summer heat, and tempered the tropical glare; and that the warm sunshine softened the harshness of the easterly stream of air, and sweetened its bitter tang. The brightness of the actinic rays made every drop of water spark and sparkle like crystal or brilliant; it flashed diamonds into the curl of every wavelet, and fired the iris sheen of the peacock body of the fly and the glint of its white wing.

This 'composition of causes' was part of the explanation, I believe, but only a part; it was the negative part, but not the causing cause. It explains why the trout were not put down by the adverse angling conditions; it does not explain

* But see above (p. 28) on the two nor'easters.

why they rose and took. It could not be the whole or the main account of that day's angling; for the rise and the take continued when the sun was low, and setting, and set.

The day-long rise and take were not due to the trout's appetite, nor to anything special in the artificial fly, nor to any hatch of natural fly, nor to the state of the water, nor to wind and weather; they were not due to anything visible and tangible in the trout or their environment. We are bound therefore, it would seem, to refer it to a mass impulse, which would come under the heading 'psychological factor', as explained above. The familiar, brief daily rise probably comes under the same heading; but on the day in question for some unknown reason the rise was unusually vigorous and long sustained.

Collective or mass impulses occur in human society. Thought-transference between individuals or members of a small group takes place; and thought-transference is often the precursor of the common impulse. In time of war or national tension telepathic communication of feeling and desire occurs, and shows in panics, triumphs and other stirrings of the general mind and will. In all such phenomena the ordinary modes of individual apprehension are temporarily suspended or transcended, and are superseded by broader currents of thought and will.

Collective or mass impulses occur in nature over a wide field; the most obvious forms are mass movements, like migrations, and the most significant forms are those, like the spawning impulse, that are exhibitions of purpose and the mass-mind. The angler says to himself, "The sea-trout will be up at the end of the month. I must have my tackle ready, and plans laid." He is counting on the mass-impulse and the mass-mind. The migration of migrant fish has parallels in widely different fields. We find it among birds, crabs, locusts and lemmings. The most marvellous of all is the migration of eels. Eels leave their home in the Saragossa Sea and make an incredible Odyssey from the ocean through our seas into our rivers and streams and streamlets and canals. Why do they do it, and how are they taught? To call it a mechanical reaction is to pile Pelion on Ossa, all to no purpose. Who or what gives the signal for their return journey, and guides it? On some dark, wet, autumn night the homing instinct grips the eels; they cross damp meadows, and slip silently downstream from river to sea, and then from sea to ocean, and thus home again to the Saragossa Sea, to mate and die. It were incredible, but that it is scientific fact. It were impossible, but for the psychological factor in the pattern of sub-human life.

In the beehive the migration impulse appears at swarming-time; but the whole life of bees seems conditioned by collective impulse and ruled by the psychological factor. Many have written well about the bee; but for poetic insight and philosophical penetration Virgil's account in his fourth Georgic of "the heavenly gift of ethereal honey"* stands apart. Virgil kept bees and studied them, and speaks as if he loved them, not merely as a theme for his magic poetry, but as a marvellous spectacle ("*admiranda spectacula*"); and it is a marvellous spectacle to see a new swarm filing into their new quarters, like a Guards' battalion under orders, the many working as one, under the common impulse to live together under rule, and build, repair, and work for one another and posterity.

Virgil wrote† that some say that God pervades all lands and seas and the boundless sky, and that bees partake in the divine mind. In the sixth book of his *Aeneid* (lines 724ff), Virgil speaks for himself, and says much the same thing, and says it boldly, and gives it universal application. A few lines after describing the murmur of the bees among the lilies in the summertime he says that Spirit within sustains ("*Spiritus intus alit . . .*") the sky and earth and sea, the moon and stars, and that Mind, interfused throughout its members, moves the whole mass ("*totam mens agitat molem*"), and mingles with its mighty frame.

Virgil's words have never been forgotten; they have influenced thought for two millenniums; the scientific advances of our day have not out-moded them, but rather

* "*aerii mellis caelestia dona*", line 1. † Ibid., lines 219ff.

have underlined their truth and illustrated it. What the bee said to Virgil, the trout says to the thoughtful angler; for the psychological factor in our angling experience is part of that 'mind-admixture' of which Virgil wrote. A supersensible basis of sensible existence is needed; it is needed to explain human life; it is needed to explain animal instinct. "*Spiritus intus alit . . .*" Spirit within sustains it all. Most thinkers would admit the truth of the words; the difficulty is to apply them fairly in particular cases. A mass movement to migrate and spawn and continue the species commends itself to our intelligence; it is purposeful; it is a phase of the general trend of terrestrial evolution; but can we accept a mass movement in trout to rise on a particular day, and be hooked, and perish? In other words, does the assumption of a psychological factor in the rise really help to explain the angling experience described in Chapter I?

I think it does. Once a collective impulse, due to circumambient Mind, is granted, the broad pattern of design is established, and difficult details can be accepted as we accept the cats and rats and otter of the inspired artist of the sacred monogram in the Book of Kells. Evolution shows us in many fields vestigial impulses that were useful at an earlier stage of development, and have outlived their use and purpose. There is much that is dark and purposeless in the migration of eels; its broad pattern is vestigial, a survival from the days before the great subaqueous convulsions that have made the bed of ocean what it is. There is much that is dark and purposeless in the dawn and dusk flightings of wild duck, in the ceremonious vespers of rooks and starlings, and in the ordinary matutinal rise of trout. It is sufficient to know that a collective vital impulse postulates collective mind. The impulse to take the angler's fly is not an impulse to suicide; it is an impulse that relaxes or weakens ordinary inhibitions, no doubt for some good biological purpose. It is therefore quite possible that the common rise of trout when there is no obvious reason for it, like a hatch of fly, is itself a vestigial impulse.

The peculiarity of the rise on the King's River on the

21st of June, 1939, was its long continuance. I have recorded the facts, but do not pretend to offer a full explanation. The clear sky, the bright sun and the keen air may have contributed; atomic energy, for all I know, may have contributed, or that curious pull postulated by the 'sol-lunar' theory. We may call it a form of midsummer madness, perhaps touched off by seasonal changes in the trout's *physique*. Whatever the impulse was, it was communicated to a large number of trout for a long time in no ordinary way. I have known things like it on the western lakes, but never on the same scale, or for so long a period. Whatever may have been the full explanation, part of it, I feel sure, was non-mechanical; something remarkable of a psychological nature occurred in the trout-world in that stretch of water; their responses were quickened; their inhibitions were relaxed, and my best day on the river was the result.

CHAPTER III

SPRING SALMON IN THE DUBLIN DISTRICT

IN the Irish angler's year salmon and trout angling combine well. Our salmon are at their best, broadly speaking, when trout are at their worst, and our trout are at their best when the quality of salmon is beginning to decline. Corrib trout, taken in February on the trolled minnow, and sent to the Dublin market, are 'snakes', most of them. Liffey salmon and Boyne salmon, taken on the opening days* of those rivers, are lusty and strong, and glitter like bars of silver. Our springers are noble fish, excelling those of the summer and autumn in size and fighting qualities and table qualities. Many of our trout are 'in the pink' by April; but they do not reach perfection till June or July.

Dublin's fair city deserves a passing word of tribute. It is a fine centre of fishing and thinking. Is there any other metropolis in which the angler can catch a salmon, and twenty minutes later be dining with the dons in cap and gown at the high table of a University. It has been done in Dublin, and it could still be done today. And if in the foregoing statement 'shoot a wild duck' were substituted for 'catch a salmon', the statement would still be true. Indeed in the latter part of August and September,

* The opening day of the Liffey is now 1 January, of the Boyne 1 February.

with time allowed, all three feats might be done in a day.

The Liffey and the Boyne with its tributary, the Blackwater, are the themes of this chapter. The salmon angling in these rivers is colourful and readily accessible; it adds not a little to the panorama of Irish angling. We begin with the Liffey. The recent installation of hydro-electric works at Pollaphuca and Leixlip has altered the character of the river, and for anglers the chief point of interest is the question: has the electrification altered the salmon angling for better or for worse? I fished the Liffey regularly through the years of transition; and while I cannot offer a final answer to that question, I have some observations to make which may contribute towards an answer; for it has been most interesting to watch the gradual transformation of Anna Liffey from a quiet medium-sized river, which turned a few mills, into the motive force of a hydro-electric system which supplies Dublin and district with water, light and power.

The River Liffey rises in the Dublin mountains only thirteen miles from the sea, as the crow flies, but it makes a circuit of over eighty miles before entering the sea in Dublin bay. It is tidal up to Island Bridge, where stands the club house of the Dublin University Boat Club, overlooking the weir. The net fishing at the Island Bridge pool used to be valuable; but it was overfished (so anglers thought), and it declined in value year by year, and was recently acquired by the local Salmon Anglers Association. There is a little angling in the tidal waters, and salmon are occasionally taken in the higher stretches of the river; but Island Bridge downstream and Lucan Bridge upstream are the practical limits of worth-while salmon angling. An old friend of mine had it from his father that to take a salmon in Lucan demesne or higher upstream was a rare event. There are several weirs between Chapelizod and Lucan, and by the time the running fish reaches Lucan Bridge his first *élan* is spent; he is beginning to stale and is less inclined to take the lure.

In former days the movements of the migrant fish* were

* I never met a sea-trout in the Liffey, though there are considerable and very early runs of sea-trout in some of the east-coast rivers, notably the Swords River. Kelts are said to be rare. I have taken three in a day at Lucan.

entirely decided by the rainfall. If sufficient rain fell to bring down a flood or a fresh, they moved up; if not they stayed put. The electrification of the river has changed all that. There is now a daily fresh, and runable water almost without intermission. The fish can now run at will. In consequence there is more fishing than formerly; whether there are more fish caught, or more fish to catch, are nice questions. I fished for several years under the new conditions, but no two years were alike; no definite trends were in evidence, and the data were insufficient to form a reliable opinion as to the net effect of electrification. I have heard that in very recent years summer grilse have begun to run in the Liffey. That is a very interesting development that may well be due directly to the daily flow of turbine water; and if the run of grilse establishes itself, it will add greatly to the angling amenities of the river. In former days salmon angling in the Liffey petered out at the end of April, or early in May, and summer grilse were few and far between.

The transition from occasional rainfall floods to daily turbine water made anglers wonder whether turbine water has the same physical and chemical properties as a flood of natural rain-water. The current looks the same, and the bait behaves in the same way in both mediums; but some anglers think that the fish are not so responsive in turbine water.

There used to be a large amount of 'free fishing' in the Liffey near Dublin; but some of it has recently been acquired by the new Association. Such fishing is not 'free' in a legal or technical sense. The term 'free fishing' simply means water, not known to be preserved, or known not to be preserved. In such waters the angler 'fished and found out'; and only rarely was he turned off. The meadows at Chapelizod were 'free', and are so still, I believe. 'Free', when I fished it, was 'the Wren's Nest'. This is a sporting pool, consisting of a weir and two or three runs, immediately opposite an old inn of that name on the Strawberry Beds road to Lucan. Fifty years ago strawberries were extensively cultivated in this warm and sheltered valley with its sandy soil. The farms that grew them were rendezvous for picnic parties from the city, and offered shilling teas with, in the season, a plate of strawberries and cream. The picturesque name for the road has outlived the industry.

Two incidents at the Wren's Nest pool stand out in memory. I once drowned a fish there. He was a fresh-run salmon, fifteen pounds in weight. He struck the bait with his tail, and foul-hooked himself in the tail. He raced upstream, and there was nothing I could do about it. He turned at the torrent under the weir, and shot like a flash downstream. The current was fast and strong, and in a few seconds I was master. As soon as the pull came on his tail, he was paralysed; his head was downstream; his tail was upstream, and he could not right himself; the current was too strong for him; his gills and his fate were sealed. I reeled him up, a dead-weight, slowly; and when he reached me, there he lay in the water at my feet helpless, dead, drowned in his own element.

One morning towards the end of March I had fine sport at the same pool. It was the day of Archbishop Barton's enthronement in the Collegiate and Cathedral Church of St. Patrick. The enthronement was in the early afternoon, and it was my duty to be present; but I had the morning free. It was a balmy, gracious day; the March lamb had vanquished the lion; and the air was champagne. I reached the Wren's Nest soon after 11 a.m., and found conditions perfect. The sun shone; the breeze was light and southerly; the water was clearing after a flood, and a shoal of fresh-run fish was resting under the weir. I put up a two-inch gold devon, and took three fish in quick succession; and then my time was up. The pool was nowhere near fished out; water and weather were still all that angler's heart could desire; it was the chance of a lifetime; but I had to go. The struggle between pastoral duty and piscatorial inclination was sharp, and the memory still is poignant. Years afterwards I had the temerity to tell His Grace why I remembered the day of his enthronement. He was a good sportsman, and congratulated with me on my three pre-prandial salmon, and condoled with me on the afternoon catch that was not caught.

The best-known stretch of the Liffey for salmon-angling, and perhaps the most productive, lies below Lucan Bridge between Hill's cloth mill and Shackleton's flour mill. A good part of this stretch lies immediately beside the Strawberry Beds roadway. You can stand actually on the side-path and cast, taking care not to hook the passers-by. The children on their way to school stop and look on, and ask, "Have you caught a fish yet, Misther?"; and their mothers, going to Lucan to shop, basket in hand, are no less interested; for angling news in Ireland is 'hot news'; it has top priority after horses. The capture of a salmon at Lucan is known at Chapelizod within two hours, and *vice versa*. If you are in a fish, a gallery gathers, shouting advice and encouragement. "Hould him, Sir. Don't let him away. Mind those bushes. Watch that tree. He's bet. He's coming in. Give him the butt."

It is a handy spot to fish, if you are out for fish, and not for privacy. There are no fields to cross or awkward stiles. You just park your car, put up your rod and fish away; and if you are lucky and catch a fish, you have not far to carry him; a few steps and he is in the boot of your car, provided there is no war on, or oil crisis in the Middle East.

It is a handy spot for the local poacher, too. He soon learned the hours of the tenant of the fishing, and adjusted his own operations accordingly. One day I came down earlier than usual when I had the fishing; and there was my brave poacher on the job, with bicycle beside the road, all ready for instant flight. But there was no flight for him that day; for his bait was stuck fast in Garnett's tree on the far side of the river. This was a sunken tree under the far bank; it took its name from a tackle-shop well known to generations of Dublin anglers, whose proprietor, a sportsman and pleasant companion, was alleged to have done well out of the snag that bore his name. The poacher's bait is still, I doubt not, in Garnett's tree. The poacher, an old soldier, got the edge of my tongue; he promised amendment of life. He promised never to fish there again. He borrowed a new trace and bait from me, and went off to pastures new.

This stretch when I first knew it was 'free fishing' and had been so time out of mind; but all good things come to an end. One year on the 1st of February, then the opening day, half a dozen of us anglers were spaced along the river bank, casting our devons and collies. Then the squire of Lucan, a cultured man, of ancient Irish family, took a hand. I admired the way he did it. The fishing was his; but his rights had not been enforced. It was not a pleasant job for a man in his position. He did not leave it to an agent, but came down in person and took our names and addresses. It was a dramatic little scene, and it had the desired effect. No proceedings were taken, of course; but subsequently I wrote and made an offer for the fishing which was accepted; and I rented it from him and his heirs for more than twenty years.

During this period the Pollaphuca dam was built to contain the upper waters of the Liffey and of the King's River, already mentioned. When the Power Station was in action, the turbine water began to come down daily. The effect on the fishing was considerable and, in one year, remarkable. To find the river fishable every day, no matter what the rainfall of yesterday was a novelty and a continuing joy. Previously we often never knew till we reached the river whether there would be any fishing, or not. In a dry spring weeks would pass without fish having a chance to run; but now the Power Station was giving us fresh water and a good current every day.

The first or the second year (I am not sure which) in which the turbine water came down was the *annus mirabilis* of the Lucan stretch; it yielded thirty salmon to one rod in the three months, February, March and April. A Liffey angler who took half a dozen salmon in the season would be well satisfied, as a rule. Thirty fish was beyond the dreams of the most sanguine of Liffey anglers. It was one of the war years; there was no petrol for private cars; and one made the journey to and from Lucan by bus. To carry a spring salmon to the bus was quite an undertaking. One day I had three to carry. The locals helped at the Lucan end; but one had to be one's own porter on de-bussing at O'Connell Bridge in the heart of the city. There was nothing for it but to carry the three fine fish, each neatly trussed up head and tail, across the noble thoroughfare. The guards (police) stopped the traffic, and the citizens of Dublin, who love a salmon as they love a horse, looked on approvingly.

That year stood alone; it was a flash in the pan, so far as my experience went. The turbine flow of water gave more fishing, but on the whole it did not give more fish. From the salmon angler's point of view there are drawbacks to the daily fresh and almost continuous flow; and the chief drawback is that the salmon are kept on the move all the time, and are not allowed to rest. Probably the explanation of the 'wonder-year', mentioned above, was that the Power Station was not in full production; only some of the turbines were working, with the result that the supply of water down each day just suited the rather placid flow of the stretch; enough water came down to send a fish or two up each day over the weir below without sending them on a through-passage over the weir above. In subsequent years all the turbines were working; a larger head of water came down each day, and the fish tended to run through. In all rivers the run of salmon is apt to vary greatly from year to year for reasons, at present unascertained, but which have no connection with local events in a particular river. The world supply of running salmon seems to vary greatly from year to year. The broad, permanent effects of electrification on a particular river must be judged over a series of years. The effect of electrification on the Liffey salmon angling is, as I write, in doubt. Time and the records of the Salmon Anglers Association may show.

And now northwards to the historic River Boyne. The Boyne made history nearly three centuries ago; it helped to mould pre-history two to three millenniums ago. Stand on the hill of Tara, and look northwards towards New Grange and the valley of the Boyne, and you are looking out on the richest lands of Ireland, richest in soil, in memories and in archaeological remains; and those remains link the country intimately with the main stream of ancient European civilization.

The Boyne fishing is thirty miles and more from Dublin, but Dublin anglers make light of the run. They like to leave their hospitals and Inns of Court and lecture rooms and offices, and get right away for one day in the week. The Boyne is further afield than the Liffey, but is better fishing, and holds better fish. The Liffey salmon is good, but he tends to be long for his size. The Boyne salmon is one of the best in the country; he is short for his size, has deep shoulders, is shaped like a bent bow, and is as strong as a horse. His average weight is 16 to 18 lb., according to the *Angler's Guide* (1957 and earlier editions). The Boyne can provide more fishing, especially fly fishing, than does the Liffey, over a longer course; it is a bigger and wider stream with a fuller head of fast-flowing water.

The Boyne rises near Edenderry and enters the sea below Drogheda; it has a course of some seventy miles, and is fed by several large tributaries. The principal salmon angling is between Navan and Slane and Oldbridge. The tide reaches to Oldbridge, some three miles upstream from Drogheda. Near Oldbridge a fine Georgian mansion, named Townley Hall, with a superb staircase by Francis Johnston,* in Olympian aloofness surveys the River Boyne and the river of time. In the narrow leafy lane that descends the hill just east of Townley Hall,† on 1 July (O.S.; 12 July, N.S.) 1690 King William on his white horse held the council of war that decided the fateful issue of the Battle of the Boyne. The left-wing of his army forded the river, and how heavily-laden infantry, under fire, could do what no peaceful angler

* F. Johnston (1761-1829) designed St. George's Church, Dublin, the Chapel Royal, the General Post Office and other Dublin buildings.

† Time has not left Townley Hall untouched. The mansion and the estate have recently been acquired by Trinity College, Dublin, and under the new name of the Kells-Ingram Farm will, it is hoped, advance agricultural research and knowledge.

would willingly attempt today has long puzzled me. July is a wet month, a month of floods and freshes; the river is broad, and to cross it even in low water would be a hard and dangerous task; the river bed is rugged; the current is rapid, and the holes are deep. "Trust in God, and keep your powder dry" — that famous Order of the Day would not be easy to observe in full in crossing the Boyne water.

A military historian has very kindly considered the difficulty, and he offers the following two-pronged explanation, and very reasonable it seems: (*a*) the infantry crossed at Oldbridge, but in the tidal water, and they waited for low tide, and (*b*) in those days the Boyne was wider and shallower than it is at present. The Boyne owes its present character to the Boyne Navigation Company, which operated from about the end of the eighteenth century; it made the canal, referred to below (p. 49), built 'ramparts', and confined the river to its present banks.

The Boyne below Navan winds through some of the richest pastures and most fertile tilth in Ireland; it skirts prehistoric barrows and the burial grounds of ancient kings; chief of them is the enormous communal sepulchre of New Grange, which dates probably from the Middle Bronze Age, and is one of the largest megalithic structures known. These structures testify to the wealth and importance of the district in those far-off days. The stones of New Grange, many of them, are profusely carved with spirals, meanders and other art-forms, which two millenniums later Irish artists were to express in other mediums, above all in the superb illuminations of the Gospel-books of Durrow and Kells.

When the Boyne opens* it is often too high to fish; you can hardly find it, let alone fish it. It is over its banks, spreading like a lake far and wide over the rushy water-meadows. When it first becomes fishable, there is little use for the fly rod; the spinning rod and heavy baits have it all their own way. Beginning with three-inch silver devons, the angler works down, as the water lowers and clears, to

* Now 1 February; up to a few years ago 12 February.

two-and-a-half inch blue and silver with its taking flash, and thence to two-inch gold; and when that stage is reached, it is time to think of changing over to the fly.

And here I must touch on a controversial matter, the law of the *medium filum*. That law was strictly observed when I first fished the Boyne, and it was part of the angler's code of honour not to trespass beyond the line. Today the law is in some stretches more honoured in the breach than the observance. The keen young angler on the far bank with his American reel and helped by a following wind drops his bait at your feet, too close to be safe or pleasant, across eighty or ninety yards of water. The change in practice is due in part to the vast improvement in the casting power of reels, which has outstripped (dare I say it?) the improvement in manners and consideration for others. On a narrow river like the Liffey the *medium filum* could not be observed without serious loss to both sides, and there, and in similar waters, by common and mutual consent in the joint interests of both banks, the letter of the law is disregarded, and both banks gain, and gain equally. That cannot be said of a broad river like the Boyne; in many reaches it is neither necessary, nor fair, to cast into the other man's water and take the other man's fish; and by doing so the one bank gains at the expense of the other bank.

Among the famous pools and reaches and fisheries of the Boyne should be mentioned Blackcastle, Dunmoe and Slane. The Blackcastle fishery extends for two miles on both banks. Its records for seventeen years (1920-36) are given and tabulated in the *Irish Free State Angler's Guide* (3rd ed., 1937), p. 178. They should be studied by all who wish to know some facts about the annual run of fish. The fluctuations are enormous, and their unpredictability shows what a deal remains to be found out about the habits and movements of *salmo salar*. The figures *per annum* range from 337 fish in 1927 to 40 fish in 1932, and from 251 fish in 1935 to 49 fish in 1936. The six years 1920-5 yielded a total of 1,163 fish, while the six years 1929-34 yielded a total of only 337 fish, the exact number taken in the one year 1927.

Dunmoe I knew well; it is a fine open piece of fishing water, about a mile long, well diversified with sharps and flats and weirs. It is some four miles from Navan, and the four miles seemed forty the evening in wartime when there was no petrol for us, and I had to 'cycle' back to catch the bus in Navan, somehow managing to fit on the bicycle my rods and tackle, three fish totalling sixty pounds in weight, and (occasionally) myself. Salmon are too lordly and patrician a fish for the plebeian bicycle; they are not happy on the handle-bars; they slip off the carrier; and if you tie them to the frame, your legs cannot get fairly and squarely to the treadmill. Nominally I cycled back to Navan; actually it was a four-mile walk with the bicycle serving as wheel-barrow for my *impedimenta* for most of the way.

Along the eastern bank of Dunmoe runs a low hill, or esker,* which gives welcome shelter from the sour east winds of April. Here the river is flanked by the remains of the derelict canal, mentioned above (p. 47), now the home of a myriad moorhens. To get to the river you must cross the canal by a frail plank, all that time has left of the lock-gate. Here is the Lock Pool, a good pool for the fly when the river is low, but unproductive in high water. A tiny church with a peaceful graveyard looks down from the hill. There, too, is a modern mansion surrounded by trees; cock pheasants crow in the plantations, and occasionally one will spread his strong wings and glorious tail, and glide, as if in conscious majesty, across the broad river.

On the western bank stand the ruins of a moated castle that in the days of the Viking invasions dominated and defended Dunmoe. Behind the castle, as far as eye can see, roll the rich pastures of County Meath, where calves, born in Kerry or the mountainy west, complete their 'sad Odyssey' and fatten for the English market. In the broad, sloping pastures, bordering the river, fat cows and fierce-looking steers (Heaven send the angler there be no bull amongst them!) roam at will, or rest among the gnarled

* Eskers are mounds or stretches of post-glacial gravel, common in the valleys of Ireland.

and haunted hawthorns where the fairies feast at night.

The Castle marks the upper limits of the Dunmoe fishing; here are rapids which in falling water may yield a fish. Some two hundred yards downstream is the Moerings Pool, a fast-flowing glide of water above a low weir, one of the best holding pools. A fish took me there at dusk. He was a 'banker', slightly red, but tough and strong. He weighed twenty-five pounds and he played for just twenty-five minutes. He would let me reel him to my feet, and then bolt straight across the river and bump the far bank. Then slowly back he came, only to repeat the dash till his strength gave out. Why does a salmon's strength give out so soon? Their average fight of 'a pound a minute' is not good considering the boundless energy they absorb in the sea, their streamlined shape, and the incredible feats of gymnastics they perform. The Erne River before the electricians harnessed it used to tumble into the Atlantic near Ballyshannon. The Assaroe Falls the spot was called; and it was a fine sight to stand there when a run was on, and watch the lordly salmon climbing almost vertically up the wall of torrent water. You would think they had a heart for any endurance test, and would never give in. His stay-at-home cousin, the brown trout, that has never had to rough it much, and that has never known the rich feeding of ocean, is, pound for pound, the better fighter of the two. Compare this stout Boyne salmon, twenty-five pounds in weight, who gave up after twenty-five minutes, with the brown trout, say fifteen pounds in weight, whose story is told below (p. 130); he was undefeated after a stern struggle lasting for two hours and a half. The same holds at the lower levels. Many a five-pound grilse gives up in five minutes. I cannot see a five-pound trout in good condition giving up so soon.

At a pool without a name lower down in the Dunmoe stretch an unusual thing happened one fine and frosty morning in early March. The sun was gaining power; but the frosty nip was in the air still; the water was bitterly cold, and the reeds and rushes at the water's edge were stiff with hoar-frost. I was wading through them, breaking the thin skin of crackling ice, and spinning as I went. All of a sudden I saw among the reeds a few yards ahead of me a sight that made me rub my eyes. "What's that, Paddy?" Paddy looked, and Paddy gasped. Sure enough, it was the back fin and broad tail of a big salmon sunning himself in the shallow water right up against the bank. "Show me the gaff, Sir." "Nonsense, Paddy," said I, "he hasn't done anything to us." Paddy's face fell. He was mortal keen to get me a fish; and here was a gift of the gods. Like Juvenal's enormous turbot, *ipse capi voluit*;* it wished to be caught.

Thinking the fish was sick, I crept up to him, and passing my hand under his body gently, I tickled him, as one tickles a trout. He was clearly in the pink of condition. I passed my hand under the whole length of him, and he did not stir. Was he asleep? Do fish sleep? Paddy came up quietly and did what I had done. For quite a time we stayed there, admiring and fondling him. Then Paddy went too far, and took hold of his tail. With a mighty thrash and smash our salmon drove out into the middle of the river, and Paddy nearly went with him.

We ought to do right for right's sake, and not for what we get out of it. Often virtue is its own reward, and has to be. But there is justice in things, as well as right; and no theory of disinterested virtue measures up to the facts. I suppose that fish had to go back to the Boyne; but he had left a debt behind him, and I frankly admit that I fished for the rest of that day with a glow of conscious virtue, and the North Briton's 'lively expectation of favours to come'. Alas, I went home empty-handed, and I could almost hear Paddy saying to himself, as I settled with him, "An, sarves ye right!" *Respice finem*, Paddy. Wait for the end of the tale. The rewards of virtue are slow, but sure. Next week when my Boyne day came round, the justice of things was strikingly vindicated. At the very self-same spot in the nameless pool just above a weir, my gold devon was

* Juvenal, *Satires*, IV, 69. Part of the fisherman's flattering address to the Roman Emperor, when presenting his fish, *spatium admirabile rhombi*.

sweeping round in a graceful curve, when a lovely fish, twenty pounds in weight, took it and met his fate.

St. Columba (*c.* 521-97) seems to have held somewhat similar views. St. Columba was the soldier-saint of Ireland who founded the famous monastery on the island of Iona, and from that centre helped to convert the Picts, and did the ground-work of the Irish mission to Lindisfarne and the north of England in the seventh century. The Saint was knowledgeable about salmon, and is twice credited by his biographer, Abbot Adamnan,* with second sight about them; and in both cases, may I say it with all respect, the Saint seems to share the angler's healthy joy in the capture of a *large* fish. The first incident may have concerned a Boyne salmon; for it occurred "*in fluvio Sale*", which, according to some commentators, is an Irish river in the Navan district. If so, it might well have been the Blackwater, which runs through Kells where St. Columba founded a monastery; Kells, after the sack of Iona by the Vikings in A.D. 805, became the seat of authority of the Columban order.† Other commentators, however, locate the river in Scotland. Wherever it was, some hardy fishermen on the River Sale had taken five fish in their net. "Cast again," said the Saint, "and you shall at once find a large fish which the Lord has provided for me." They did so, and they drew ashore a salmon of amazing size ("*mirae magnitudinis esocem*").‡ One can almost see the concertina action of the narrator's hands. The other incident occurred for certain in Ireland. The Saint was staying on Lough Cé in County Roscommon with some companions who were fishermen. They wished to go fishing; but the Saint restrained them for two days, saying there were no fish in the river (the Boyle). On the third day he let them go, and they took two salmon of extraordinary size ("*rarissimae magnitudinis*").

Boyne angling today has its special charm and its distinc-

* Adamnan, *Vita Columbae*, II, xviii, xix.

† The Book of Kells was probably written to commemorate this event.

‡ *Esox* today is technical for a pike. In antiquity it seems to have been used for any large fish, even a sturgeon. There were no pike in Ireland in those days.

tive features: the holding pools and reaches are long and wide; the current is mostly full and strong; fishing rights are understood and respected; the fish are of fine quality, and to take one of thirty pounds weight is no uncommon event. There is great variety in the fishing. One must be reasonably active and prepared to walk a good deal to take full advantage of it; but walking is a pleasure there; the setting is that of a rich and prosperous countryside, happy, smiling and historic. The Boyne angler fishes in wide, open spaces, and feels as free as air; and to the tired city-man his day on the Boyne is a weekly tonic, fish or no fish.

To balance the picture here is an account of a famous piece of water in Navan itself, not two hundred yards from the Boyne. It, too, has tonic qualities; but the medicine is in tabloid form; for here all is narrow and compact and on a small scale. Yet it is a pool where great fish and great thrills and great experience are to be had. The pool is called the Mollies. Ask why? and I reply, Well because it *is* the Mollies. The old cricketer was asked, "Why do they call it a *yorker*?" And he replied, of course, "Because it *is* a *yorker*." All Navan anglers and most Dublin anglers know the Mollies, its name and fame. It is a pool on the Blackwater (not to be confused with the southern Blackwater), a tributary of the Boyne. It flows down from Kells, and joins the Boyne in Navan town, and the Mollies is the first considerable pool above the junction. There is no noticeable difference between a Boyne fish and a Blackwater fish; and presumably it is a matter of chance whether a running fish would turn right at the junction into the Blackwater, or continue up the Boyne to Trim. They say that salmon return to their native rivers to spawn. The dogma must be, broadly speaking, true; for rivers have their distinctive types of fish. Does the dogma, one may ask, apply to tributaries? Would a salmon parr from the Blackwater, when full grown and returning from the sea to spawn, seek to return to the tributary, or would the main river do as well? The latter alternative is probably correct. For nature acts by general tendency, and not always with mechanical precision.

De minimis non curat lex; the law of the land does not bother about details, and the same would seem to be true of the law of instinct.

Here are some facts and figures about the Mollies, which show what a curious pool, or rather group of pools, it is, pointing the contrast with the Boyne. The total length of the Mollies is one hundred and eighty yards; its average width is nine yards, and it narrows at the waist or gut to five or six yards. It stretches from Spicer's flour mill on the south bank to Elliot's saw mill on the north bank. Every inch of it is fishable at some height of water, and every inch of it may hold a fish. Three rods on either side, six in all, can fish comfortably in high water; in low water two rods a side is enough. A total of twenty-four fish was taken from the pool on the opening day (then 12 February) some years ago. Since that time structural alterations have been made in the fish pass at the upper end, and the fish can run through more easily. As a result the Mollies, though still a good holding pool, does not hold as many salmon as it did. In the good old days whenever you looked at the water in March or April, you would see a salmon turn. The pool was often overcrowded, and there was one very sad year; a great run of fish early in the season was followed by a long, long drought. The pool was full of fish; the water got staler and staler, and furunculosis appeared; in that confined space it spread like wildfire; it was pitiable to see those noble fish a prey to the dread disease; there they were all around you, blotched, gasping, dying, and dead, by the score. On one day eighty infected fish were removed from the pool.

On the north bank the Mollies is approached through the saw mill; through the tree trunks and piles of planks and heaps of sawdust you make your way to the accompaniment of screeching saws; and the cheerful men working them shriek 'tight lines' to you. The approach on the south bank is quiet, unusual, and almost romantic. The angler enters by a private garden gate through the courtesy of the owner, and crosses a trim lawn and passes through gardens of flowers and vegetables which run down almost to the water's edge. Snowdrops and scillas and a few hardy crocuses welcome us when we start work in February; rows of sturdy cabbages and broccoli, somewhat the worse for the January snows, are bravely struggling to live and grow and thrive; the gardener is pottering about doing odd jobs, but rarely losing sight of the river; and if he sees your top joint bending, he will soon be at your side, in case you need assistance, as expert with gaff as with spade.

It is a strange situation, is it not, to be fishing here for salmon in a private garden in the heart of a country town? The fishing is varied and interesting; in one hundred and eighty yards of narrow stream you have an epitome of all the main types of angling for spring salmon from a bank. Here is fly fishing, direct casting and Spey casting, except at the very beginning of the season and in very high water. Here is bait fishing except in very low water. On the great majority of fishing days both fly rod and spinning rod are in use, if not everywhere, at least in parts of the pool. The water, too, is well varied; here you have broken water and smooth, sharps and flats, fast, medium and slow; and each variety of water calls for some special knowledge or knack or skill in handling fly and bait.

Stand at the head of the Mollies in the shadow of Spicer's mill up at the weir, and if a run is on, you will see the big fish slipping up the ladder one by one or jumping at the falls and often tumbling back. Immediately below the weir is a seething cauldron of water in which it is futile to fish. Walk down a few yards on the narrow stony path between the river and the mill-stream, and you will find the current slower and the water fishable. Now the river widens, and leaves a stretch of slack beside the main current, and the slack water may hold a taking fish. At the bend is a sheltery pool, known as the Ladies Pool, where the current slows, and many a fish is taken in medium water. At the outflow of the Ladies Pool the banks narrow like a *v*, and the current gathers pace and pours into the gut which is the strangest feature of the Mollies. The gut at its narrowest is barely twenty feet from bank to bank. On the north side is a vertical face of rock at the base of which a narrow pathway, often flooded, winds. On the south side the mill-stream rejoins the river under a flimsy wooden bridge. The gut is a curious geological freak, but a great spot for a fish. In the lowest water there is current in it. A big conical rock sticks up in the middle of it, and salmon rest behind the rock, beside it and in front. Here a young bride, who had never fished before, hooked and killed a salmon thirty pounds in weight; her reputation as an angler was made; and, perhaps wisely, she hardly ever fished again.

Below the gut runs a fifty-yards stretch* of relatively quiet water, and that is the only stretch fishable in a high flood when the river comes down brown. At the tail of this stretch a long sunken wall, well beneath the surface, running diagonally down across the stream, carries the water to the saw-mill sluice. This wall is a famous lie for fish, and a famous place for losing baits. Below the wall is 'The Pool', a grand holding pool, where the river broadens, slows down, and then gathers momentum and hurtles over the weir where the Mollies ends.

The Mollies is a gold mine to dealers in angling requisites; there is hardly an inch in it where you cannot lose a bait; there is hardly an inch in it where you cannot lose a fish, no matter how well he is hooked and how strong your tackle. Rocks are everywhere, submerged, unexpected rocks, cruel catchy rocks. It is no place for a novice at angling. It is no place for a novice unless he is dead keen to learn the job. If he is keen to learn, and prepared to pay the price, the Mollies will teach him. It is a hard school, but a good school; it teaches the whole curriculum. If a man can fish the Mollies, he can fish anywhere. When he has lost a few pet baits, he will learn to read in the swirl the exact position and the depth of the sunken rock; he will feel his way to the delicate touch and the nicely-directed fling that brings the bait round, just skirting the snag where the big fish can see and take it. He may, as the gillie said, "shtick in the Republic" a time

* On the north bank of this stretch Mr. T. Lynch caught five salmon weighing 106 lb. in an hour's fishing on 16 February, 1929. *Angler's Guide to the Irish Free State*, p. 180 (5th ed., p. 208).

or two; and that will teach him when to reel fast, when to reel slow, when to raise the bait, and when to lower. He will learn the art of releasing a bait; he will learn the virtues of the 'traveller'; and if the 'traveller' fails to release him, as often as not an angler on the far bank will see his trouble, and come along like a Good Samaritan, risking his own bait, and will hook the other's line, and pull and release him and set him free.

The Mollies is the place to learn the salmon's ways; there are plenty of salmon in the pool as a rule; they often show, and close at hand. The taking rise, the sulky rise, the turn of the running fish, the uneasy sideways fling before the rain, the prospecting leap of the fish just up over the weir — these are all to be seen at close quarters, often all in the one day. In some lights on some days the way of the salmon with the fly can clearly be seen here only a few yards off; up he comes, and looks, and turns away down; up he comes, and looks, and looks once too often.

The Mollies teaches the whole art of playing your fish, and grassing him; but teaches the hard way. The angler who hooks a salmon on a broad river or a lake has usually time to look about him and to mend his hand. With a hooked fish on the Mollies there are no second chances. The angler must be 'on the spot', and his tackle must be all in order, and his handling and management must be correct from the word 'Go'. They take so near you; there is no free line; they feel the vibration of the check instantaneously, and the vibration sets them mad, if they are that way inclined. He may be half the length of the pool away before you realize you are in a fish; and the first mad rush of a mad spring fish, just up, with the sea lice on him, is almost always to the narrow gut. A hooked fish will rush almost ashore there, and the danger of fouling the line round a rock is great.

If he takes in the lower portion of 'The Pool', the weir is the danger; he is liable to go over either in his first alarm or in his last despairing effort; and if he goes over, a loss is certain — at least so I thought till this year. My first fish this season took at the lip of the weir, and went straight over; it was impossible to stop him and impossible to follow him. I was for giving up, and cutting my losses and my line; but my friend William, a fearless young athlete, would not hear of it. So I held on; my tackle was strong, and the moil of waters beneath the weir buffeted the fish, and seemed to stun him; gradually I reeled him up into the white foam under the bushes at the foot of the fall; and there he hung half in the water, half out. William did the rest; pluckily he scrambled down the edge of the weir, and luckily he was just able to reach him with the gaff.

That salmon panicked over the weir because of the very high water; but generally in ordinary water, when hooked in 'The Pool' at the edge of the weir, your salmon does not panic, and gives you time to plan. But leave nothing to chance, however quiet he seems. By draw or by pull coax him away from the weir. The 'draw' is one method; the 'pull' is another. You draw from above the salmon, you pull from below him. The draw can be most effective, if he has not been frightened at the strike. In the draw the reel must be very quiet, quite still if possible; if it revolves rapidly, vibrations from the check travel down the line and excite the fish. If you can manage to tighten on him without alarming him, take a step upstream, holding the line firmly with a finger on the reel, but ever ready to release it if he fights. Probably he will respond to the gentle pressure and follow you upstream. If so, repeat the movement, moving ever slowly, steadily, and without a jerk. A big, fresh fish, if handled skilfully, will be amazingly docile; and if you can draw or lead him fifteen or twenty yards upstream before he turns restive, that is half the battle won. The other method, the pull from downstream, is more primitive, but it can be most effective. Essential to its success are that (*a*) you should be well below him, and (*b*) he must be reasonably fresh and not tired. Given those conditions your fish should react to the pull like a thoroughbred.

The Mollies is a fine school for the young salmon-angler, and it can be a great comfort to the old. Not a few elderly folk fish it year by year with a feeling of gratitude. A day on the Boyne with its far and strenuous casting and its long walks from pool to pool may be too much for him; but on the Mollies he can enjoy his sport, and take his weekly tonic of fresh air, change and exercise, with little walking, no discomfort, and a fair chance of a fish or two.

CHAPTER IV

THE BREAK

IT is rather a disgrace to break in a fish; but breaks occur in the best regulated angling; and I will begin with the story of a remarkable break. It is a tall story, and I preface it with the solemn declarations that, with Izaak Walton, I love virtue and angling, and that I have long loved fishing and philosophy, trout and truth. What I am about to relate really did happen to me; my story is strange, but true. The incident happened forty years ago; but it is as clear to memory as if it happened yesterday, and a solicitor friend witnessed it. My story has much in common with the famous Greek story of Polycrates, but goes one better.

Polycrates, tyrant of Samos, had fabulous wealth, health and happiness, and all that heart could wish; he grew uneasy; for extreme happiness (so the Greeks of old taught) provoked *Nemesis*, the jealousy of the gods. He sent to Delphi to consult the oracle about it. "Throw into the sea your most valuable possession," replied the oracle. Obediently the king rowed out into the Aegean, and threw overboard his diamond ring, set with pearls and rubies. A few days later there was a state banquet, and the king and his nobles gathered in the banqueting hall. A turbot was served on a golden dish, was carved and distributed; the king opened his portion, and out on his plate rolled his diamond ring, set with pearls and rubies; the king turned pale; he now knew the worst; the gods were jealous and they had refused his sacrifice; his doom was sealed.

The fish element in the Greek story is plausible enough; for fish do swallow glittering objects, and do get caught, and are bought and sold, and a turbot is a dish fit for a king; but that that turbot should have swallowed the king's ring and been bought for the king's table was a remarkable coincidence. Still all fish can see and move and swallow; the agent that restored to me from the waters my prized possession could do none of these things.

I was fishing from a boat on the Upper Reservoir at Bohernabreena, a few miles from Dublin, with my friend, Mr. Bindon Scott, a solicitor, now with God. In those days the Rathmines Town Council was in being, and controlled the fishing and performed the functions that now come under the Dublin Corporation. I had three small flies on my cast — my pet Red Spinner on the bob, a Silver Priest on the tail, and what the middle dropper was I forget, and it is of no account. There was no nylon then; we fished gut and nothing but gut. Gut in *some* respects, not *all*, was better than nylon; but gut needed soaking, and if worked or knotted dry, it would crack or draw and weaken; in consequence breaks occurred often. Moreover the trout were gut-shy, and we fished fine. I was casting from the stern of the boat; my Red Spinner was bobbing attractively in the surface ruffle; a fish rose; there was a short, sharp jerk, and nothing more happened. It was a break. Most anglers have known that anguish. The fish had broken the fly from the cast. Presumably he broke it with his mouth; but sometimes they lash out at the fly with fin or tail. In such cases the fly is usually left sticking in the fish, and he goes off to the rubbing stump, or engages the help of the tench, reputed the doctor-fish.

Nothing like that occurred in this case. That trout broke my Red Spinner somehow from the cast; but he did not go off with it in mouth or fin or tail. Neither I nor (so far as I know) any other angler met that trout again; yet the fly he broke off is back in my fly-box. That clever trout somehow managed to break my Red Spinner from its gut-point, and spit it out or otherwise get rid of it instantaneously. How he did so I cannot imagine; but he did so; it was a strange happening.

A stranger happening was to follow. I recovered my fly against all the chances in a scarcely credible way. I tell it in the words I wrote in the correspondence columns of *The Irish Angler*,* Summer Number, 1939.

"We were in deep water; by all the chances that fly, falling from the fish's mouth, should have sunk to rest and rust at the bottom of the lake. But no; fate and the long arm of coincidence willed otherwise; for as I, slowly and sadly, drew the cast back into the boat for repairs, first the bob-point, flyless, then the middle dropper, and the Priest on the tail — when the silver tail-fly came up over the edge of the boat, to my amazement there, caught and safely held, hook in hook, was my lost Red Spinner."

Such incidents are food for thought. Anglers, as a class, are not superstitious; they are too objective and purposive and hale and healthy for sickly superstition; but they do meet strange events and coincidences that defy the laws of mechanism and probability. Only rarely can it happen that a trout will break off a fly without it sticking in some part of him. The chances that a small fish-hook sinking in an open lake would catch and hold in another small fish-hook must be infinitesimal; yet both these improbabilities took place. I say nothing against mathematical probability and mechanical causality in their place and province; but there are "more things in heaven and earth", and anglers know it to be so.

Mechanism and materialism are dumb before facts that are part of the A, B, C of the angler's every-day experience, such as the herd instinct in fish, the simultaneous rise of trout all over a large lake, the simultaneous cessation of the rise, the migration of migrant fish, especially eels and

* *The Irish Angler*, a promising journal, was one of the first casualties of the war.

salmon and the directed movements of salmon in still water. These events and other manifestations of animal instinct are inexplicable without the assumption that animals at times apprehend in supra-normal ways, and that assumption appears to involve pervasive mind, and a spiritual basis of terrestrial life.

Take the case of the salmon in Lough Conn. Practically all of them enter the lake from the Pontoon end; they come from the Moy via Lough Cullen, and the vast majority of them make their way along shore routes, well known to local anglers, to the River Deel at the northern end of the lake, near Crossmolina. There on a fine Saturday in late April or early May you will see a fleet of small craft, spinning or trolling or fishing* for salmon. In a river the movements of salmon are semi-mechanical; the current, pressing against their shoulders and flanks, directs them; but when they leave the river and emerge into a vast expanse of still water, what is their compass then? How does a salmon find his way fairly quickly from Pontoon to the Deel? The set of the waves changes from day to day and hour to hour, and even if we may suppose constant currents under-water, these can hardly be sufficient to guide the traveller along many miles of deeply indented shore-line with multitudes of creeks and bays. We may call it *instinct*; but we are none the wiser unless we go on to ask, With what are they instinct? In what alchemy have they been dipped? These scaly machines that are super-mechanical — with what alchemy are they instinct? Stream-lined, oiled and almost frictionless, they shoot up the sheer torrent, and glide like shadows through the tossing flood.

The tale of one 'break' has led me far afield into the mystery of animal instinct, and I must come back now to my humdrum task of explaining why breaks occur, and how they may be avoided. The transition is not so abrupt as may

* In this usage, which is quite common among those who know and is a well-deserved tribute to the superior excellence of the fly-rod, to 'fish' is a specific term, used exclusively for angling with the artificial fly for game fish; it can thus stand in antithesis, as here, to trolling and spinning and other such ways of taking fish, which, though perfectly legitimate and often necessary, are still, to the artist, inferior methods; see below (p. 135).

appear at first sight; for in studying the break and how to prevent and cure it, we are studying a remarkable phase of human intelligence that links man to the instinctive behaviour of lower forms of life, and yet sets him on a higher plane.

To break in a fish is a humiliating thing; it is a reflection on our knowledge or our skill; it is a mark of imperfection in our angling, and our minds are set for perfection. Man can see through his imperfections in thought and action, and can try to set them right. He has an ideal towards which he works consciously; that is his privilege and prerogative, and it sets him immeasurably above the creatures of instinct.

The angler who has never thought systematically about the break would learn the essentials from the following little experiment. Take a length of twine, thin but sound, in your two hands and pull both ends steadily apart; probably it will not break, no matter how hard you pull, provided you pull steadily. Now leave a foot of it loose between the two hands, and pull with a jerk and a snap; probably it will break like tow. The game fish, if convinced, takes with a snap. The keen angler, if awake, strikes at the chuck felt or the rise seen with an involuntary jerk, and if he wishes to avoid a break, he must remember and allow for those two distinct forces, the fish's snap and his own strike. It is the combination of the two that strains and may break the cast. The first precaution is to tone down your strike by means of the checked reel. Adjust the check to the strength of the cast you are using; but always leave the reel free to turn at the strike; keep your hand from it, and make sure your coat-sleeve does not catch the handle. I know some anglers of experience who do the opposite; they stop the reel at the strike, for fear of losing line at the strike, and not being able to tighten on him quick enough. By and large their method does not pay on the limestone lakes; you may net a few pounders you would otherwise miss; but when the fifteen pounder comes along, he will break you, and you will not even have the satisfaction of knowing that he weighed fifteen pounds.

If there is a weak point anywhere in your tackle, the fish will find it out. If one of your flies, and only one, is loosely attached, he will come for that one, and will leave the others. There are several possible weak points, and all should be constantly checked, viz., (*a*) the line itself, especially if tapered and more than two or three years old, (*b*) the attachment of the cast to the line, (*c*) the attachment of the droppers to the cast, and (*d*) the attachment of the flies. Dry the line every night after wetting; the waterproofing soon wears and weakens, and once the silk begins to go, it goes quickly; if you cannot trust it to take a hearty snap and jerk, scrap it at once. The cast must be shorter than the length of the rod, or if you hook on the tail you may find it hard to bring him to book. Droppers should stand out well from the cast, and should not wrap round it. I like them three inches long with a little allowance for snipping and changing flies. Looped droppers stand out well, and if the loop is inserted in a knot in the cast, it cannot run up and down.

Knots are a wonderful achievement of the human mind; they set a broad gulf between man and beast; but only sailormen and small apple-eating schoolboys can really master their intricacies. Learn them when you are young; get an experienced gillie to teach you; the essential knots are: (*a*) for tying together two strands of gut or nylon, (*b*) for the loop at one end of the cast, (*c*) for attaching the line to this loop, and (*d*) for attaching the fly. This last is the most wonderful and most important of all anglers' knots; it holds like a vice at the fish's pull, and releases instantaneously at the angler's push. When he has mastered this knot, the angler can slip a fly on and off with ease and safety, and then, and only then, can he make full progress in his art.

Test your cast every day, and oftener, and do not be content with any *pro forma* test; give the same snappy pull that a strong fish would give; the tail-fly wants watching; for the gut or nylon gets drawn and worn there; another weak point is at the first dropper, where the cast tends to hinge at the throw.

The break obviously depends in part on the breaking-strain of the gut or nylon used. It is hard to give particular advice on that matter. In general one should fish as light as is consistent with safety. The fly on a light cast is more animated; its fibres dance more attractively, and presumably it is less visible than the thicker cast. Gossamer tackle, however, is utterly out of place on the big Irish lakes; personally I prefer to err on the side of safety; you never know what you may meet. If a big trout is interested, really interested, in a lake-size fly, the size of the cast, even if he sees it, is not likely to deter him; if he sees it, it may be no more to him than the shadow of a weed. The conditions of the day have something to say to this question. If there is a fresh breeze and good wave, and not over-much sunshine, use a strong cast and big flies; but if the breeze goes light and the wave becomes a ripple, try a lighter cast and smaller flies. But I have known a very large Golden Olive on a very strong cast greedily swallowed by a three-pound trout in dead calm water. Most gillies will tell you that as a rule the thickness of the cast makes very little difference on these limestone lakes.

Breaks will happen, and there is, indeed, one type of break for which the angler cannot be held responsible, and that is the break in the hook, its shank or its barb. Steel hooks should not break, but they do break; they break in fish, and they break in snags at the forward and, particularly, the backward cast. No doubt there is a flaw in the steel, and if the angler touches fish after fish and loses them, he should look at his hooks.

It is bad enough to break in a trout; to break in a salmon is even more serious and more humiliating. In salmon angling the chances are fewer and the stakes are higher. To leave a fly or a bait in a salmon may be to lose a fish of thirty pounds weight, and to lose your one chance of the day; you might have gone home in triumph; and if you go home empty-handed, whose fault is it? "Daddy, if you go out fishing, why don't you catch fish?" That is what the youngsters are thinking, and what they say.

I have said some hard things about the break, and I will close on a more philosophic note. "'Tis better to have hooked and lost, than never to have hooked at all." Do your best not to be broken; but if the break occurs, be patient; learn your lesson; draw profit from adversity, and try, try, try again.

CHAPTER V

THE FINNEY* RIVER

THIS chapter is a tale of two trout, a loss and a win, and, incidentally, it describes an unusual type of angling in a very curious stream. The Finney River is not what its name suggests. The name would make one think of a broad, full-flowing stream with an exceptionally large population of fish. In point of fact the Finney is hardly a river in its own right, and its finny population for the greater part of the year is nil or negligible. And yet it can tell of many an angling thrill, as the following pages show.

The Finney is a link between two lakes, and little more than a link. The two lakes are Upper Lough Mask and Lough Nafooey; both lakes are long and narrow; the Finney is short and fairly straight. You may picture it as the bar joining the two strokes of the letter H. You could walk from lake to lake in an hour or less, and the going is not good. In a word, the Finney River is a short and narrow channel through the bog, through which the surplus water of Nafooey (if there is any surplus) flows into Mask. Nafooey, when I knew it, was regarded as a pike lake. Upper Lough Mask holds large trout, but it was not much fished then, because the main lake, which meets it at the causeway, fished better.

* Also spelled 'Finny'.

The Finney fishing is seasonal, and has a very short season indeed. Its fish (one might almost say, *more Hibernico*) are birds of passage. Except during a few special days at the latter end of August and September the Finney holds no worth-while fish. In a dry spring or summer the river becomes a trickle; the flats are stagnant bog-holes, which may hold a few, lank snake-like trout; and there may be a few pinkeens in the sharps; but such soft, undernourished trout are not those of which I write.

With such a short season preservation presents difficulties, and what the position is now I cannot say. When I knew it thirty or forty years ago the then owner made an attempt to preserve it, and put up a notice to that effect beside the little bridge over which the Connemara ponies clatter with their panniers of turf. He even paid a watcher. He was more interested in the shooting, I heard, than in the fishing; a letter to him brought a courteous reply, giving me leave to fish whenever I wished.

A great change comes over the Finney when heavy rain falls, and Lough Nafooey fills and spills over. The water, being filtered, does not thicken much; but the stagnant flats through the black bog-land become full-flowing slides or glides; the shallow sharps turn into tossing torrents. After, say, the middle of August the fresh mountain water, charged with oxygen, is champagne to the big lake trout in Mask, already feeling the spawning impulse. They dash to meet it and enter the little river, like running salmon from the sea.* Up they go in a day or a night, passengers to the spawning grounds on the further side of Lough Nafooey. But they rest *en route*, and if you find them in the mood, for pure *joie de vivre* they will snap at your Golden Olive or bushy Invicta or dainty Connemara Black.

*There are no salmon in Lough Mask, or virtually none; they cannot face the underground river that connects Mask and Corrib. One hundred years ago, or more, a canal was cut to join the two lakes; and it is just possible that a few salmon got up then, and have left landlocked descendants, or that a few daring fish face the underground river, which can be seen at 'The Pigeon Hole'. At any rate the locals told me that very occasionally a salmon was taken in Mask. The ruins of the canal works can still be seen; its projectors thought of everything else; but they forgot that limestone leaks.

But please do not think they are an easy prey. These are wise old trouts, and they have seen artificial flies before. Moreover they are not easily fished; it is hard to present the fly to them. Casting is cramped. Some flats are narrow slits, overhung with heather, and to work three flies down and across is not easy, and the sharps are too broken and turbulent. Look out for the pet spot where a journeying fish might rest, and look about him. Let your cast linger provokingly behind that rock; cast twice, thrice into the widening of the flat; trail the flies into the eddying currents of that backwash; and, in particular, search any sheltered water you may find.

The rising flood is almost useless for our purpose except, maybe, the first ten minutes of the rise; the full flood is quite useless; our time comes when the flood begins to fall, has fallen, and the water is clearing; then the trout can see the fly, but not too clearly, in the wine-dark stream.

What may the angler expect to take back with him? Well, he should be satisfied with two or three trout for his day's work; his bag will be heavy enough for one pair of shoulders. I once had five in a day, and their total weight was nineteen pounds; their individual weights were, in pounds, five, four, four, three, three. On my very first evening on the Finney I lost a very large trout, of which more below; and that reminds me to say two things about the evening fishing. First, if at all possible, and unless the water and weather conditions are dead against you, stay for the evening rise. Unless the flood is rising, or there is rain in the wind, or frost in the air, there is almost certain to be something of an evening rise; and even *one* rise may be the fish of your life. The other thing is this: Midges! If the evening remains warm, and the breeze drops altogether, there is a danger from midges. If a cloud of midges comes down, run for your life. No matter how good the conditions, even if the trout are rising, even if the big trout are taking, run for your life, and look not back. Lot's wife looked back, and met a bad end. Take down your rod before stings seal your eyes, and race to your car and go off.

A swarm of Finney midges are more venomous, more maddening than the ten plagues of Egypt. No trout is worth it; cut and run.

On a breezy evening in late August my wife and I first made the acquaintance of the Finney River. People had told us about it, and we came out of curiosity, not believing what we had heard. We had no expectations beyond the perennial charm of casting a line in waters new; if we could take a half-pound trout from so small a brook, honour and ambition would be satisfied — or so we thought, and we left the net behind in the car, challenging fate and fortune.

We worked upstream from the bridge, and met no response for an hour. At 'the witching time' of dusk, when the duck were flighting and lost curlew were calling, we came to the tail of a run, where the broad sharp narrows, wedge-like, into a deep flat with heathery banks deeply undercut, and in the rough, just at the tail of the run, I struck a fish, a big fish, a very heavy fish. My rod was light, and my tackle fine, and there was little I could do. There was not so very much for him to do either, but he took complete control. He raced upstream at first, but not liking the broken water of the sharps, he turned and entered the long flat. There he sailed majestically up and down, unable to run far in the narrow reach. He bored, and all I could do was to keep the pressure firm, but yielding. He jumped, and all I could do was to lower the top joint to him, to keep the line clear of the over-hanging heather, and to hope and pray that the tail-fly would not catch in reed or rush. For twenty minutes I fought him in the gathering gloom, and then he surfaced and began to tire. Meantime my wife had raced back to the car, and returned panting with the net. Alas, the net was too small for the job. He lay there at my feet, beaten; he was the largest trout I had ever seen, though the two Lough Conn trout I saw since were larger (see below, pp. 113, 130); with a full size net he was ours. I did the orthodox thing in the circumstances; that is, I centred the ring at the middle of his body, and lifted, hoping that head and tail would collapse into the bag of the net. I lifted, but head and tail did not collapse; he was too big and strong. I lifted, and the lift slackened the worn hold of the fly, and he slithered off; the rod straightened, and we were left guessing at his weight, and pondering the bitter truth of Izaak Walton's words, "Nay, the Trout is not lost; for pray take notice, no man can lose what he never had."*

We often spoke of that fish with tears in our voices. Our sorrow for that trout 'lost' (if I may style it so) in the Finney has been keener and more lasting than our joy in that other Finney trout, as good as lost, and yet restored to us, as by a miracle, after a memorable and epic fight. Before I proceed to tell that second story, let me reflect that in this and in other matters angling is a faithful mirror of life. Anglers are not the only folk who place a higher value on the prize they narrowly missed than on the prize they won.

The tale of the Finney trout I *took* centres on the bridge I mentioned above; it is one of two bridges over the Finney; turf-cutters use it; it carries the track that links their bog to the main road. It is a solid stone structure, and it needs to be; it has two spans, and in a flood both spans are taxed to capacity. Anglers like bridges, and so do fish. Anglers like them; the bridge is the obvious place to leave the car, and you can often choose your side there to suit the direction of the breeze. True, in our weaker moments we do not always relish the proprietary notices posted at the bridge: FISHING PRESERVED TRESPASSERS PROSECUTED. Here memory takes me to a similar bridge in Scotland; it was a wild spot, too; but Scottish wildness is never quite so wild as Irish. A pine tree overhung the bridge, and on the tree was posted the following notice:

TROUT ANGLING FORBIDDEN
HERE ON SUNDAYS

What was I to do? This was a Friday. Rod and everything necessary were in the car. The small stream was in perfect order after a night's rain. I had a couple of hours to spare. I looked at the notice again with the cold scrutiny of a

* *The Compleat Angler*, I, v.

logician. Fishing forbidden on Sundays—surely that is tantamount to saying that fishing is permitted on other days. Any Irishman would read the notice as a *Nihil obstat* on week-days. Fish and find out — I acted on the principle, and was rewarded with half a dozen fat little half-pounders. My decision was pragmatically justified, and that evening when I reached my destination the receptionist at the hotel had some doubt as to whether there was a room for me. "Well," I said to her, "I have a trouteen to spare," and I slipped one across the counter. It worked wonders, and I got my room.

Subsequently I talked over the notice with a friend who knows Scotland and Scottish logic better than I do. He said, "No; you made a hasty inference. That notice in its primary intent was an advertisement of Sabbatarian principle. It contained one definite prohibition, and that was all. There was nothing between the lines. You had no right to read permission there."

Which of us was right? If my friend was right, I apologize to the Scottish laird for my trespass and my logic.

And now come back to Erin and the Finney River. I was saying that fish like bridges. Why they like bridges I do not know; but certain it is that a good trout is often taken immediately above or immediately below a bridge. The bridge pool at the Finney was above the bridge, and it was an ideal resting-place for a travelling trout; for immediately below the bridge is a fifty-yard stretch of rocky shallows, which in a flood became a raging cataract of broken water. Trout fresh up from the lake find the torrent a tiring run, and they gladly rest in the comparatively quiet water of the pool above the bridge.

All anglers on the Finney start there. This was the day on which I took the five trout whose weights were specified above (p. 70). The two three-pounders I took from the bridge pool in the morning. I worked upstream to Lough Nafooey, and on the way captured the two four-pounders. The best was yet to come. After lunch I began again at the bridge pool. The water was still high, though falling, and was pouring like a torrent through the arches of the bridge. To my delight I was soon fast in another big trout. I was fishing three flies, lake size, on a medium cast of two x gut, which will stand a fair strain, but must not be overtaxed. He was a strong mettled fish, and he kept the centre of the stream. I moved well below him, and put on all the strain I dared; he responded as a fresh-run salmon does. As I pulled downstream, he went upstream, and thus to my great relief I worked away from the dangerous bridge, and well clear up to the next fall. There I fought him for ten minutes, and he began to tire. I gave him the butt, but his head was still down. I pulled him round a few times, but, try as I would, I could not swing him into the slack water. He was too tired to respond as at first to the downwards strain; and at each swing round he slipped back a yard or two; and presently we were back where we started, ten yards only above the bridge. Then fate took charge; the rest had to be. He was not played out by any means, but he could no longer fight both the current and me; and it was clear that he meant to make down towards the lake from which he had come. From the bridge my wife and small sons were watching the struggle; they saw his intentions, and seizing stones they plumped them into the river immediately behind him, and frightened him upstream for a few minutes. Then as the pressure of the current and the pull of the line continued, he threw away the lesser fear, and with one determined plunge he hurled himself into the seething moil of waters, and was swept away down through the arch on my side. The reel screamed; away in a flash went ten yards of line, twenty yards, thirty, forty yards, and then there was silence, and I thought that all was over. There was I, rod in hand, above the bridge, gazing through the span; and below the bridge were my cast, my fly, my fish and forty yards of line, and in between raged a tossing sea of foaming water. What could be done? A thought came to me, as I looked at my top joint, and measured the distance with my eye. Yes, it nearly reached. The arch was over ten feet from north to south, and mine was a ten-foot rod. I had splashed through the archway in low water and I knew that the footing was firm and good. I shouted to my wife to run round to the lower side of the arch. Holding on to a fence with one hand, I leant forward and lowered the top joint and stretched it out to her. She could touch it, and, straining, could just grasp two inches of it. It was a frail hold indeed, but it was enough. Feeling like Horatius confronting the yellow Tiber, when the bridge went down, with a sigh and a prayer I committed to the torrent, not myself, but my Hardy rod and reel, hoping for the best, fearing the worst. Rod and reel fell like a stone. My trusty helper held on to the tip manfully. I raced round, took it from her hand, and retrieved the rod. Reeling in, I recovered line, and to my amazement felt the trout still on. Forty yards lower down I drew him from his holt under the bank, and aided by fortune I swung him downstream into a backwater, where the net ended the long, fierce fight. He was a five-pound fish of noble proportions, broad-shouldered, short and deep, a fighter worthy of death in battle. Never before or since have I hooked a fish above a bridge, and killed him below.

CHAPTER VI

THE MOUNTAIN TARN

VARIETY is the salt of angling, and in the west of Ireland, to my knowledge (and in other parts of the country, no doubt), the angler can find the variety he seeks, usually near at hand. There are various types of fish and various types of fishing. Salmon and sea trout and brown trout are there, to say nothing of pike and perch and char; there are rudd and dace and rarer species. They can be caught from boat or bank, in lough or stream or full-flowing river, in fresh-water and, some of them, in brackish estuary. Footsore and leg-weary after a heavy day or two on the river, take a few days' boating on the lake. Then boatsore and cramped and tired of the continual rocking that pursues you in your dreams at night, give the mountain tarn its turn. You will enjoy the change and exercise and the exciting scramble. The fishing itself is usually dull and unrewarding, and the tarn trout, for the most part, are of poor quality compared with the trout of the limestone lakes; but the climb is great fun. It is a young man's fun, of course; but it is great fun in youth to be climbing up and up the airy mountain with the prospect of some hours' fishing on top of the world in that tonic air.

Choose your day for it, if you can. Do not go in a biting east wind, or when heavy rain threatens, and the clouds are piling up at the south. At the tarn itself there is no shelter for a wren, and if it rains for long, you will be wet through, your sandwiches will be mush, and you will get no fish. The sun is all to the good, if there is not too much of it. You want a breeze but not a gale; and the force of the wind needs careful study before you decide to go; for a smart and lively fishing breeze on the lake will probably be half a gale up above. You will know the day when it dawns; it usually comes in July or August after several days of high wind; the glass is still low, but rising; it is a day of light, fleecy clouds overhead; white clouds are evenly distributed all round the horizon; there is no air-stream anywhere; the lake is not dead calm; but the breeze on it is a mere ruffle, not enough to stir the lazy trout. You will scorch your ears, and spoil your complexion, and break your heart on the lake. That is the day to try your luck on the mountain tarn.

The highest tarn I ever fished was Kelly's Lough on Lugnaquilla, the highest mountain of the Wicklow range. From the summit of the Lug on a clear day the view is commanding and exhilarating. To the north are the Mourne mountains and the Carlingford range, like a jagged saw. In the far nor'east the Donegal mountains, with Muckish and Errigal, are dimly seen. The western and southern heights appear; eastward, across the sea is the coast-line of Wales, dominated by Snowdon and Snowdonia. The Lough, if memory serves me, is about one thousand feet up, under a beetling crag, a haunted spot. I fished along its rocky shores in a high wind, and took a trout, one pound in weight, black as ink.

Not so high up in the world, but equally eerie, are two tarns, known as the Dirks, up in the hills on the western side of Lough Mask. Thirty years ago you drove your car a few miles southward from Tourmakeady, parked by the roadside, and climbed on your two feet to a height of some seven hundred feet up a broken causeway, built for turf-cutters, but cut to ribbons by the winter torrents. The causeway has been repaired, and now, I am told, you can drive to the tarns.

The two tarns lie there side by side, both fed by the one

set of streams, and sharing, it would seem, the stream that gives access to the lake. The trout in the two tarns are of different types. The larger tarn is deep, and has shelving sides, and the trout are small, soft, many, white-fleshed and hungry; it is hardly worth fishing. The smaller tarn is shallow; you can wade about in it; weeds and reeds abound in it; you cast into the weeds often, and your tackle must be stout; for you may have to drag your fish through them. These trout are of the lake type, and, no doubt, have been spawned by lake-dwellers; they are short for their size, stocky, strong and pink-fleshed. I do not remember any large ones taken, but I remember more than one fine basket of a dozen or more up to one pound in weight.

And now for a group of tarns to which no roadway or even path gives access. They are not marked on the map; they are little more than glorified horse-ponds. You must take a gillie, if you go, for the first time; you would never find them yourself, and the locals will not direct you, or will misdirect you; there is mystery about them. They are tucked away in folds of the high moors, where landmarks are few. An angler might pass within fifty yards of one of them, and not see it. The natural features of the place are no sure guide to them; they are off the main lines of the water-courses, the gullies, ravines and streams. They do not nestle at the foot of beetling crags, like Kelly's Lough. They are perched on the crest of a ridge. Geology, no doubt, can account for them with the help of the Ice Age; but they look like geological freaks. Mother Nature seems to have gone striding over the moors, setting them down like cups and saucers at random here and there.

There is a group of four or five of these cups, or rather saucers, high up on a ridge in the moors within a radius of one mile. One of them was known as the One-eyed Lake. The locals said the trout in it had only one eye. I fished and had no response, and concluded that the trout in it had not even one eye. Another of the tarns had a bad name; it was considered dangerous to fish for some reason or other. "Beant the One-eyed Lake there's another wee lough, Sir;

but I wouldn't throw a line in it, if I were you. There's a sort of a creature living in it, like a water-dog [an otter], only as big as an ass." Such stories create and foster and reflect the atmosphere of the district. Even on a calm and sunny day, these high moors have a haunted look; and when the winter winds are howling down the pass, one would not wish to be up there alone. Then these moors *are* haunted. Solitude and melancholia people them with ghostly monsters, with water-sprites, the Pooka or the Piast.

Over moors and uplands like these, W. B. Yeats — poet, dramatist, and man of letters — roamed in his younger days with rod and flies, or "humbler worm". Yeats is one of the few great poets of our time who have fished and put their thoughts about fishing into verse. In his honour then we will make a short pause here; for these mountain tarns look out on the district known as 'Yeats's country'. We will in thought lay down our rods, rest on this tussock of dry and springy heather, relax, enjoy the tonic air, the tart fragrance of the moors, and the blue of the Atlantic out there; and we will talk about Yeats and his angling and the meaning of his curious poem, *The Fisherman.* We shall perhaps see more in our own angling, and understand it better, when we see it reflected in the creative crucible of a poet's mind.

Yeats refers to his own angling several times in his writings, and his poems owe a good deal of local colour to Ben Bulben, and the moors, mountains and mountain streams of Connemara. As an angler he was, one would surmise, no mean performer. He certainly understood angling technique. No novice would have noticed and remembered the angling details he gives. He notes the black of the stone, just beneath the surface of the water, with the white froth above it, and speaks of "the down turn" of the angler's wrist, as he drops his flies beside it. Then, too, the bodily activity, the muscular exertion, and the hard exercise involved in mountain angling meant much to him. No camp-stool by still waters, nor peaceful canal for him, no angling in the valley or on the levels of the lake. His angler is always "climbing", usually at dawn, up the hill or mountain side. His angler is physically fit, an "upstanding" man, as Yeats was himself, till, as he tells us, his writing unfitted him. He wrote:*

> I leave both faith and pride
> To young upstanding men
> Climbing the mountain side,
> That under bursting dawn
> They may drop a fly;
> Being of that metal made
> Till it was broken by
> This sedentary trade.

I saw the poet often, and in memory I still see his massive head and fine figure, bowed by the weight of years and thought. My clearest recollection connects him with the sports of youth. We met at the annual cricket match on Parents' Day. Other fathers had squeezed into their white flannels, and were facing the demon bowling of their sons with hilarity and hope. Yeats joined in the fun in his own way, taking his enjoyment at second-hand. He would sit by himself for much of the time on a bench under the elm trees, by way of 'watching the game'. What game was he watching? I wonder. His head was bent almost to his knees. Surely he was looking through the mirror of the present to the past, re-living his own youth, recapturing some of its activities with joy and pride?

In some such mood, perhaps, he wrote *The Fisherman.*† It is a difficult poem to fathom; it is neither mystical nor weird; but it is strange, *sui generis*, and baffling. The mists of morning twilight hang around it; the language is simple, but the meaning is complex and obscure. The poem is by an angler, about an angler, and it has some deep meaning for anglers, if we could find out what that meaning is.

* *The Tower,* London, 1928.

† First published in *The Wild Swans at Coole*, London, 1919. In a later collection, *The Tower*, London, 1928, there are unmistakable references to *The Fisherman* (e.g., section III).

The Fisherman begins with this portrait:

> Although I can see him still
> The freckled man who goes
> To a grey place on a hill
> In grey Connemara clothes
> At dawn to cast his flies,
> It's long since I began
> To call up to the eyes
> This wise and simple man.

The portrait is not a passing fancy, but a poetic creation, deliberately and repeatedly 'called up' for some purpose from time to time. It is not a self-portrait, though it clearly must reflect some part or aspect of the poet's angling. It is an ideal figure, says the poet, that does not exist; but of course it does exist; and that is part of our puzzle. The Fisherman is a real ideal. This freckled man in Connemara homespun, climbing up rod in hand, with a cast of flies looped loosely round his hat, and spare flies stuck in the lapel of his grey coat — we meet him in the flesh any and every day in these parts (though not often at dawn*), and we exchange the angler's greeting, 'tight lines', as we pass. He is so real that we may call him 'Freckles' without disrespect.

The poet conjures up Freckles and shows him to us, and at once apparently leaves him aside, and goes off at a tangent on his own sorrows. He will write for his own race, and his own folk will understand and appreciate. But do they? Not at all. Far from it. The bright vision fades into drab reality. Enemies, cowards, the insolent, knaves, drunkards, low wits and clever clowns, the destroyers of wise men and great art — such are the real people he meets. He scorns to write for such as these, and, for audience, he comes back to his Fisherman, Freckles the Angler, his ideal-real. He draws the portrait over again, freckles and all, and depicts the man dropping his flies in the stream beside the frothy stone, and declares:

* Yeats finds the dawn irresistible.

Before I am old
I shall have written him one
Poem maybe as cold
And passionate as the dawn.

That, in outline, is Yeats's poem *The Fisherman*. Its scene and setting are those of this wild, upland district where we sit. Look again at the prospect. That yonder is Yeats's country. There is Sligo Head in the distance. See the coast-line and the surf, and the blue ocean, no longer blue, but whipped up now by a grey west wind into grey white-capped combers. Before we examine the meaning of the poem, take note that its scene and setting are real, and not imaginary.

What does the poem mean? What did it mean for the poet? We may rule out the suggestion that it is mere description or scenery. Yeats's Fisherman is no mere literary ornament, no conventional angler, conventional adjunct to the purling brook or echoing waterfall. *The Fisherman* for all its restraint is a passionate poem. Freckles, the ideal-real, sprang from some deep, recurrent experience associated by the poet with his angling; for whatever else he may intend by the poem, Yeats certainly says by it in effect, "If all my readers were like yon climbing angler, they would listen to my words." Why did he pitch on *angling*, of all occupations? Why did he idealize the *angler*? It could not have been an accident. He must have found something in his own angling that answered a felt need. Was it objectivity, the sense of control by the object? The artistic imagination is in special need of such control, and values it. When one's sense of reality is perturbed, and the line between the real and the imaginary wavers, and perhaps the point approaches when "nothing is but what is not", a day on a river is a wonderful cure. It takes us out of ourselves, and confronts us with the comforting blank wall of something not ourselves, to which our sensing, imagining, thinking and action must conform. The sanity of the angler's outlook commends angling to the sick in mind. Some *say* they can imagine a Banshee, the

Pooka, or the Piast. Some *say* they can imagine Cosmic Evolution without a Cosmic Mind. But however strong may be a man's powers of imagination, he cannot gaff a salmon that is not there. The poet can 'create', as we say, a character or event or drama out of thin air, and body it forth in words; but he cannot create a trout on the end of his line; and if he thinks he can, he will soon be disillusioned. The fresh air, the open spaces, the physical exercise, the nature of the occupation and the objectivity of the chase combine to make angling a sedative and a general tonic for the occupational dis-ease of the man of letters; and if W. B. Yeats had found it so, as seems probable, it is no wonder that in later life he turned back nostalgically to the sport of his young and active days, and idealized it.

The concluding lines of the poem give one a glimpse of a somewhat wider and deeper explanation, carrying a stage further what was said above. Yeats was never a weakling, and one does not associate him with sedatives, tonics and medicines for the soul; but there are hints here that Yeats had found in his angling, and had projected into his ideal angler, something of that deep experience, known since Aristotle's day, as *catharsis*, emotional purification. The "simplicity" of his wise man points that way, and so does his description of the "one poem" he will write. And if Yeats did find some measure of *catharsis* in his fishing, he was not the first, nor the last, to do so.

"I go a fishing," said Simon Peter,* when he was perplexed, out of touch with his ideal, and perhaps beginning to sink again. He went and fished, and after a dark night he met the Ideal in the dawn light. "I go a fishing," says the cross angler to himself. He got out of bed on the wrong side, and the porridge was burnt; and he hates his work, and is disappointed with his home, and despondent about himself, his character, his health and his prospects. Out he stumps with rod, reel, book and creel, a prey to envy, hatred, malice and all uncharitableness. In an hour on the river he forgets

* John xxi, 3.

it all, and he comes home at nightfall, happy, hopeful and light-hearted, forgiving, forgiven, re-created, a new man, emotionally purified.

In the greater part of *The Fisherman* clearly there is no *catharsis*. The poet's emotions are as nature willed and made them. His portrait of the ideal angler whom I have dared to name Freckles (because he is so real) was conceived in a mood of rebellion. Freckles stands there a witness to a poet's scorn. Scorn gives temporary relief to over-charged feelings, but scorn gives no *catharsis*. But here is a poem within a poem. In the last four lines Yeats looks forward to writing a second poem addressed to the same ideal-real angler. He will write it before he is old, and it will not want the force and fire of youth; but there is a difference; for it will be emotionally purified, "as cold and passionate as the dawn". If I interpret correctly that rich and challenging phrase, then the *catharsis* desired by the poet for himself and his readers will appear in that poem-to-be, penned without heat, in "calm of mind", all black passion spent.

So much for the poet, and his angling, and his poems to the angler. Now back to the prose of life. We must rise, rested, from our heathery couch, take up our rods again, and return to our group of mountain tarns.

Two of these tarns, like the two Dirks, differ widely in respect of trout nutrition; but unlike the Dirks these tarns have no access to a big lake; they are virtually self-contained, though not self-sufficient. One of them is called Barna; the other has no name, and does not deserve a name. The nameless tarn teems with fingerlings, hungry little trouteens, about three ounces each. They rise in all weathers and on the slightest provocation — poor things they have to do so. On a mild, taking day, with a light west or sou'west breeze, put up three small flies, a red, a blue and a silver-tinsel on the tail, and you will get them, three at a cast. "They do be fighting one another to get at your fly, tearin' the feathers off it," says Mick. You could take fifty or a hundred in a morning; but they are good for nothing. Put them in the larder over-night; next morning they have gone soft and flabby, and you may throw them out.

The nameless tarn has one use, and one use only. If there is a lady in your party who has never fished before, and would rather like to learn, or if there is a lad to be initiated, bring them round to the shallow side of the pond; put up your oldest rod for them (the gillie will repair it next day), and set them at it; stand clear; they can come to no harm, and they are almost certain to catch a little trout or two; and what a thrill that will be for them. It may make them anglers for life.

Barna, five minutes walk away, is a different story. I must linger on it, and will take you there, if you will come. It is worth a visit by the expert, simply for the size and nature of the trout it holds. They are amazingly large, but ill-shapen and of poor quality. They are caught there, two pounds and three pounds in weight, and larger ones, with dorsal fin and broad tail showing, may be seen sailing about. The locals tell of a sporting squire of fifty years ago who stocked the pond with rainbows. An expert from the Fisheries Department would not hear of that explanation. These trout, he said, are natives, bog-trout in bog-water; importations could never have survived in the hard struggle for existence up on these barren moors, over which the golden eagle and the raven fly.

His explanation was this — and it applies to other tarns, similarly placed. Barna has only a small catchment area. There is a small heath-covered hillock on its western flank, and a corresponding fall-away on the east; there is no steep declivity on either side. No stream pours daily in or out. See for yourself; you can walk round it in twenty minutes. The water seeps in at the upper end and seeps out at the nether end in the ordinary way. In heavy rain, of course, there would be a heavy intake for the duration of the rain, and a strong outflow or even a torrent, and that deep cleft in the black turf* shows its normal path; but otherwise there are no steady streams or streamlets in and out; there

* *Anglice*, peat.

are no head-waters, properly so called; in ordinary weather there is only a trickle of water in and out. In consequence there are no facilities for spawning; the trout spawn as best they can, or remain spawn-bound; the ova have little protection; most of them are gobbled up in the shallow margins of the tarn; if any escape and hatch out, the alevins would miss the steady flow of fresh water that they need, and few would grow up to a healthy maturity.

On my first visit to Barna I took Mick with me, and, from him, on the way up I learned a good deal, and about more than fishing. We drove to a height of some four hundred feet above sea level, parked the car at the roadside, and made ready for an hour's trudge up the wet mountain. It was a warm day, and we travelled light. Waders are not necessary in the summer months; they are too heavy and hot for comfort. Tennis shoes and grey flannel trousers are better. The flannels will give protection from the briars and nettles and clegs or horseflies on the way up; roll them up and tuck them in when you reach the tarn, and two legs are a pair of nature's waders. Mick carried the rods and tackle, the lunch and mackintoshes.

Leaving the road we struck down a boreen and passed a thatched cottage; a dog barked; the curtain across the window of the living-room twitched and was half drawn aside, and we caught a glimpse of a man's face, obviously not too well pleased to see us. I could not understand it at all; for the folk are so friendly and chatty as a rule, and the fishing-rod is an almost universal passport of goodwill.

Our way led up a sheltered ravine where dragonflies as big as birds were hawking up and down, or perching and posing on the sun-baked rocks. A small stream chattered and clattered down the centre of the ravine; we heard it, rather than saw it; for it was almost hidden from view by the tall bracken which grew to the water's edge. Up we climbed. Suddenly Mick plunged through the bracken, like a cocker spaniel on a hare. He peered hard into the stream, and then gazed at the low mound beside it. "What is it,

Mick?" "Come here, Sir, and look. See, it's all there. That's the 'worm', down there in the water. That mound is the rest of the still; and the turf for the fire is set all around. They're going to do it this very evening, sure as a gun. That's why we got no welcome at the farm. It's a bad business, Sir, that poteen. The Guards have a right to put it down. No good comes of it. Half the families about here are destroyed and poisoned with it."

Mick's words did him credit, and his show of righteous indignation was impressive; but I had my doubts. He certainly knew what to look for, and where to look. The average man would have passed that still a hundred times, and would never have seen it. Mick certainly knew a good deal about the 'industry', and for the rest of our climb he was hardly ever at my side for long. Again like a cocker spaniel he was casting about and winding in all directions, scouring the gullies, searching the tufts of heather, and the clumps of reeds and rushes and all the nooks and crannies in the rocks that might hide a bottle.

We joke about it; but it is really no joking matter. Excuses used to be made for the manufacture of poteen and the traffic in it; but there is no excuse for it today. Anglers should not encourage it. The Church and the law are dead against it, and local sentiment is hardening against it. With all the welfare organizations that exist, and the public assistance available, few families, however marginal their holdings, really need the short-lived illicit gain, and the lasting loss in physique and morale in poteen-making districts has been incalculable.

Leaving the ravine and its poteen factory, we climbed a steep heathery slope, and found ourselves on a broad plateau that commanded a view of the western sea-board, fringed with the ocean, shimmering in the sunshine.

We were nearly at our destination, but between us and the head of the ridge where the tarn lay, stretched half an acre of bog-land, which we had to cross. Not all moorland is bog; much of it is firm, hard and even stony; but every now and then, without warning, you come on these soft and yielding dips, and then you must tread warily, walking delicately, like Agag, picking your steps.

If you fish or shoot in any part of Ireland, sooner or later you will meet an Irish bog, and you will need to know the rules of bog-trotting. Here are three golden rules that hold everywhere; they will stand you in good stead, whether the rod is on your shoulder or the gun. The rules are: (*a*) Have an eye for the rushes, (*b*) Walk on the brown and the red, (*c*) Beware of the green, especially the light green. Never hurry or run, of course, and never try to cross a shaking scraw. The rules require a word of explanation; the corollaries speak for themselves.

Have an eye for the rushes. Wherever rushes grow, there will be a spot or two of *terra firma*. This is the rule of rules; it never fails, summer or winter, down in the plains or up on the moors. By 'rushes' I do not mean bulrushes or those tall lances and spears that grow in swamps or by the edges of some lakes, but the ordinary rushes, standing two or three feet high, that grow in every wettish field; the farmers cut them for bedding, and snipe feed amongst them. I do not know their learned name; but they are tough and pliant and have a pithy centre and a sharpish point. Wherever you see even one of them, you can safely place your foot.

The colour of bog vegetation is significant for the traveller, and the bog is no place for the colour-blind. Warm colours and firm soil go together. The reds and browns will almost always give you safety, if a *wet* safety; the dark greens are probably safe; but never trust the light greens. That delicate, attractive light-green hue is as treacherous as a fairy sunrise. Is it chickweed? Whatever it is, it never seems to grow save on top of deepish watery mud. It looks so safe; it is so alluring to the novice who has been floundering ankle-deep through mushy browns and reds. He sees in front of him, as he thinks, the familiar colour of good, green grass; with relief he steps out firmly on to it, and so, in the expressive phrase, "he takes the green bath". Bog cotton, with its white feathery flower (if it is a flower), used for dressings in the First World War, is to be avoided, if possible. One can never be sure of it, and it sometimes grows in very wet spots. The most serious danger is the shaking scraw. Your foot goes down and through, and you see a shudder and a rippling tremor spreading across the green surface for yards ahead. It is a shaking scraw. Do not panic; remember Agag and Carver Doone; pause and take stock; retrace your steps, if you can; if that is not possible, say a prayer, and proceed *pedetemptim*, as the Latins graphically expressed it. Feel your way daintily with your foot. Your foot may sink six inches, and find no solid support, and yet the grasses and weeds and the clinging mud itself will supply enough diffused resistance to permit a short step forward. Quick jerky movements may be disastrous. Keep the foot flat; distribute the pressure and weight; go slow, and you should escape to *terra firma* like Christian in *Pilgrim's Progress* out of the Slough of Despond, albeit "grievously bedaubed with the dirt".

We crossed this bog without difficulty, and soon found ourselves on the ridge, our destination; and there at our feet lay our mountain tarn, Barna, snug and smiling in the sunshine, like a silvery gem, framed in brown and purple. As I said before, tarn fishing is not as a rule exciting; but Barna is somewhat different; this little tarn offers features that even the hardened angler will not soon forget. The breeze had remained light and patchy; what there was of it was from the west and struck the tarn fair along its length. It was just right for the dry-fly, which is to be preferred on these small waters. If the breeze gets up, and the wave is over an inch in height, the dry fly does not cock up well, and there is 'drag'; the wet fly is better then. But this day was obviously a dry-fly day. The pattern of fly makes little difference. The trout in Barna probably see an artificial fly only half a dozen times a year; and provided it is plausible, they will not be 'choosey'. The sun was shining, and Wickham's Fancy would have done; but I had the Coachman up, and it, too, lights up attractively in the sunshine; so I left it up, and started at the western end. On Barna a natural rise is rare in daytime; but the trout are often up and waiting, though not showing. A rise here is usually a take; for the fish are hungry; and if he takes, two surprises await you, a violent take and a quick surrender. I had not long to wait; there was a wild and greedy snatch, far more violent than the well-fed, gentlemanly pull that lake trout usually give; my reel screamed and the line hissed as he raced across to the far side of the tarn. Then came the second surprise, the sudden collapse of opposition. He threw up the sponge at once, and as I reeled in, he came to the net like a lamb to the slaughter. I felt the heavy weight at the end of my line. The big fin and big black tail came nearer and nearer, and there was virtually no resistance. When I looked at him on the grass I understood the reason why: the big head and long black snaky body spoke eloquently of continual under-nourishment. Barna was never meant for trout of this size; but they are there. I have taken them up to two and three pounds weight, and have seen monsters cruising there; but I have never taken a well-shaped fish from Barna, nor anything under a pound and a half. The trout there are permanently underfed; they have no shoulders, no stamina, no heart for a fight; and if hooked, after their one mad rush, they come in quietly to the waiting net, as if glad to leave those hungry waters.

What effect (if any) does the sight of a trout, fighting for dear life at the end of your line, have on the other trout? Sometimes, it has no effect. Could it be that sometimes it starts a panic? Trout are liable to collective impulses (see above, p. 35); why should they not be liable to collective impulses of fear? When you are fishing from a boat on the lake, a trout will follow up the fly, will suddenly see the boat, and go down with a terrific splash; and then you may have to wait quite a time for another rise. Salmon undoubtedly panic, and communicate their panic. A red prawn, never seen in the sea, is extraordinarily attractive sometimes; at other times it will terrify all the fish in a pool; you can see it from above. I have wondered whether that dash across Barna by the big trout I took could have started a panic in the tarn. I did not get another rise before lunch, though the conditions continued good. In well-fished waters familiarity with lures seems to breed contempt; the burnt child does not always dread the fire, and the pricked fish does not always dread the hook; the risk run and the safety won may pre-dispose both child and fish to run the risk again. But in a small mountain tarn, rarely visited by the angler with his lures, it is quite conceivable that the panic dash of a hooked trout could put his comrades off the feed.

Failing to move them, we left them alone till the heat of the day was over. We had lunch and enjoyed a sleep on the scented heather. About four o'clock the air cooled and the breeze freshened. Changing the fly, after hard work I succeeded in grassing two more two-pounders. About six o'clock the breeze dropped, and everything went still and lifeless; and we took the hint and our leave, and made our way down to the car.

CHAPTER VII

THE GILLIE

THE Irish gillie helps to make Irish angling what it is. He is essential to visitors fishing the lake; and even a local angler who 'knows every rock in the lake' will enjoy his day more if he has with him a gillie whom he likes and who likes him.

The gillie, as a rule, is a small-holder who lives by working his farm; his fishing is a sideline which helps to balance his budget. His potatoes go down before his salmon angling has well begun, and are not dug till the fishing season is over. His turf must be cut during the season, and his hay and oats and roots need attention from time to time; and if he asks off for a day or half a day, or does not want to stay out late, he has a good reason; he appreciates consideration, and deserves it. Some gillies are employed by the fishery owner at a weekly wage summer and winter. For some less lucky ones the end of the season means the end of their job, and during the winter they take casual jobs, or hang around and 'support the bridge', and look over the parapet at the salmon turning, and 'think long' for spring and summer. A few are bailiffs, and earn ten or twenty pounds a year from Boards of Conservators for protecting the spawning streams, and asking to see your licence. It is a precarious livelihood for many of them. The fishery may change hands, and the job may lapse; and the job has its own dangers, amongst them the wealthy angler who has had a good day, and is too free with his flask.

Whatever else your gillie may do, while he is gillying he is 'on the job', and he puts his heart into it. He is your man, and as long as there is a fish to be had, he will do his level best for you. From morning to night he will keep at it, if there is a sporting chance; but if the prospects are hopeless, if the lake goes flat calm in the evening, or a bitter nor'easter springs up, you may take his word for it and rest from your labours.

He earns his wages and his tip; but he is no mere 'hired man' working for his pay; at least he should not be, and he would not be, if things between you were on their normal and proper footing. Your gillie is a craftsman, with a proper pride in his craft, expressing himself in it, ready and glad to exhibit it. Paddy and Michael were two such craftsmen; both were great friends of mine, and I think of them both with gratitude and regard. They represent different types. Paddy was all for salmon, and Michael for trout; and there were deeper differences. Paddy had no land; Michael had twenty acres; and the possession of a little land makes a big difference. Both were 'good mixers' and good company; Michael had dignity. You could no more address Michael as 'Mick' or 'Mike', than you could address Paddy as 'Patrick'.

Paddy had all-the-year-round employment at one of the big salmon fisheries of the west; he hauled the nets in the tidal waters, and he helped the angler on the river. What Paddy did not know about salmon and salmon anglers was not knowledge. "Don't bother about him, Sir; he's too near the bank; he's an old red fellow." Paddy's eye watched the position, the manner and the angle of every rise. He noted the forward drive and splash of the running fish, entering a new pool and having a look round; he noted the sideways throw of the sulky fish, and the rigid upward leap of the stale fish in the rain, falling away backward as if minded to drop downstream with the coming flood. He watched like a lynx for the head and tail turn of the taking fish. His eye caught and held and interpreted the signs. Paddy was an old soldier, a veteran of World War One. He was well trained in watching on the firestep, and listening and interpreting the signs through the long, dark hours of sentry-go. I can see him still in memory, with his smart knee-breeches of Bedford cord, his brown leather jacket with zip-fastener, and his cloth cap stuck with salmon flies of his own tying.

Paddy had no book-learning; he had few interests outside his job, and little feeling for things of the mind; in some ways he was a mediocrity; one would forget him, as soon as his services were no longer needed, only that his personality was vigorous and vivid. He was always cheerful, always hopeful, often very helpful and always complaisant. Those are great qualities in a gillie. "The pool is full of fish today, Sir." He would always start work with some such assurance; and if there is no response after a long bout of fruitless flogging, he will keep your heart up by telling you it is only a question of finding the right fly. "That tail-fly is too big and bright, Sir. We must change it. I've the very thing in my book here." And if there is still nothing doing, he will land and make you a cup of tea, or tell you a tale to make you laugh. And Paddy had his great moment when after a long, dull spell, the line straightened, the reel screamed, and the top-joint bent to take the strain. He rose to it; his composure was superb. "You're in 'im," was all he would say; but he was in command, like Wellington at Waterloo. His eye gleamed and glinted as he watched you, your rod, the water and the fish. He'ld not fuss you with directions, nor would he let you fuss him. "It's all right, Sir; don't worry; he's well hooked; we'll manage him; his head's coming up; he's tiring; watch those weeds; he's thrashing; slacken line; he's nearly done; swing him into the slack, if you can; he's coming; give him the butt; he's come." Then Paddy lets drive with the net, and the fight is over.

If your gillie is complaisant, it is no blame to him. Be thankful for it. He has to be all things to all men; it is his pleasure, and it is to his interest; it is part of his craft; he must play his man, as his man plays the fish; it is his job to see you pleased. Would it be any better, if he began by telling you, as one dismal Jimmy of my acquaintance did, that there was not a fish in the pool? To start the day without hope is to end it without fish. Should one remind one's gillie of his earlier optimism, if the long hours pass without response? It is a nice point of protocol. Personally I should be chary of doing it unless I myself were cheerful and knew the gillie well, and was sure he would take a bit of friendly chaff. Paddy, anyway, would have been equal to the situation, and I can hear his prompt retort, "Ach, Sir; they were here all right; but whatever's on 'em, they've gone on up."

He has to deal with all and sundry, the choleric Colonel, the College don, the seasoned expert, the raw novice. Now it is the beginner who can scarcely cast, and asks where he is to stand, and how to hold the rod. Now it is the lady who is out for a couple of hours, and positively must have a fish to take back to Dublin. Paddy will do his best for each and all; and we must do our best for him. He does not cross us, and we must not cross him. Fishing, salmon fishing especially, is trying to the temper. Expectation is keyed high, and failure is more frequent than success. The hunting instinct is aroused, and the instinct of combat is not far away. We strive for 'the sporting spirit' to keep these instincts in check; but even good sportsmen when they are after fish are after gain and glory; they are at the instinctive level; they are deaf to reason, and long-continued frustration 'gets them down'. Paddy knows all this, even if he does not put it into words; in dealing with frustrated anglers he is dealing with 'kittle cattle', and it is not for him to cross a cross angler, and add fuel to the flames. Complaisance is his form of silent sympathy, and it is often 'oil on the troubled waters'.

He would often ease the situation with a story; and if you had just lost a fish at the gaff — the most testing of piscatorial situations — and had taken it well, he would reward you with one of his best. He was not a born story-teller, like some Irish peasants; and often he was quite obscure. He had one about a salmon fly, known as 'Skin-the-goat'. He enjoyed telling it, and I often asked for it, but could never fathom it. "Why is it called 'Skin-the-goat', Paddy?" And he would start up with a chuckle, "There was a man, Sir, had a goat . . ." And on he would ramble for five minutes, as clear as mud, and would wind up with echoing peals of laughter, ". . . and so it was called 'Skin-the-goat'." I have often heard the story; but the etymology of the queer name of that efficient fly is still a mystery to me.

Paddy's best story was a long one; but he told it well, told it with zest, and with those graphic touches, peculiar to folk who see and perceive and think directly. It was about Admiral —— a big, stout gentleman, a good sport as a rule; but you daren't cross him; for he had a touch of the heart, and was nervous about himself, and we about him. One day he was out with my son, who was learning the trade. "Now, Mick," said the Admiral, "twenty bob for a twenty-pound fish today." At the head of the Long Pool he hooked one and lost it, and was not best pleased. Lower down he hooked another which played hard. "This is your fish, Mick, a heavy springer," said the Admiral. Half an hour passed, and he couldn't best thon fish. The pool was just above a weir. The fish tried every corner of the pool, and when he found he couldn't get off, he worked downstream to the tail, and with a plunge went right over the weir. The Admiral couldn't follow for the trees, and was fit to be tied. And what did young Mick do? He snatched the rod from his hand, jumped into the river as he was, and over the weir after the fish. He swam ashore, played the fish out, landed him, and brought him back in triumph. The Admiral didn't half like it. He took out his spring balance, hooked him up, and read it. "Nineteen pounds and a half; eight ounces short, Mick."

Paddy paused for effect. His audience thought it was the end of the tale, and were not sure of its point. Was it Mick's pluck, or the Admiral's precision? It was neither. "Well, did Mick get the twenty bob?" I would ask. "He did not, Sir," replied the story-teller, and took up the tale. "The very next day Mick and the Admiral was fishing together; and the Admiral got stuck in another big one; and was not getting on too well with him. It was a very hot day, and Mick was sweating; and he took off his coat to cool himself; and the Admiral thought he was going in again; and he got red in the face, and redder, as red as a turkey-cock; and he let a roar you could hear a mile off. 'Stay where you are, boy. I hired a gillie, not a water-dog.'" That was the point of the story. An Irishman loves a quaint comparison; and Paddy's quick imagination was feasting on the picture of Mick in the moil of waters, rod in hand, chasing his fish, as the water-dog in river or lake hunts his salmon or trout. The same feeling for the bizarre shows itself in Celtic art. On the Chi-Rho page of the Book of Kells the sacred monogram is depicted with overpowering beauty and resource; it is the supreme work of religious art on vellum. In the detail of that glorious page along with "angels and archangels and all the company of heaven" appear cats watching rats or mice, and a water-dog with a fish in his mouth.

A water-dog, by the way, is the west-country name for an otter. Otters are shy creatures; but you may see them an odd time on the big lakes. We were drifting along one of the myriad shallows that stud Lough Conn, and could move nothing. Suddenly we saw the reason why; right in front of us rose from the lake, like Venus Anadyomene from the Cretan sea, one of those grey marauders, sleek and glistening, with a two-pound trout in his mouth. Seeing our boat he trotted up over the rim of the islet and out of sight.

Paddy had one trick of speech that defied grammar and logical analysis. Royalty and editors often say 'We', where 'I' is meant. Paddy did the opposite; he said 'I' where he meant 'We'. "How did you do today, Paddy?" When he answered, "I got three fish, Sir," you would think, if you were not familiar with his idiom, that he himself wielded the rod and threw the line. He did not. His 'gentleman' cast, and hooked the fish and played them. Paddy's part was just to net or gaff them. One hears various explanations of the idiom. It may be a legacy from the Irish language, the mother-tongue of his forbears, now struggling against fearful odds for survival as a living language. Like 'you' in English, the pronouns of the first and the second persons in literary Irish admit considerable latitude in the use of singular or plural. Possibly Paddy's idiom reflects the tradition that angler and gillie are partners, and to that extent one entity; it is more probable that there is egoism in the idiom; for Paddy was not always ready to push the 'I' to its logical conclusion. He would say, "*I* got a fish," but not, "*I* lost a fish." He was agreeable to partnership in success, but not in failure. One summer he was gillying for a Colonel who was a bit of a duffer, and Paddy did not take to him. I met him one evening when the day's work was over, and put the usual question, "Any luck today, Paddy?"; and Paddy made the discriminating, but astonishing, reply, "I got two fish, Sir; and the Colonel lost four." The poor Colonel — his two successes must be shared with Paddy; his four failures were his own!

Paddy was a master of punt-craft; and his handling of the clumsy-looking vessel made it a thing of beauty, an instrument of purpose; and with his ten-foot pole, iron-tipped, he expressed his purpose as truly as does the *maestro* with his slender fiddle-stick. Those who know the punt only on the Isis or the Cam only know it as a means of transport. In Paddy's hands on a broad, full-flowing river, like the Moy, the punt is much more.

It was a joy to see this rough, tough man, with his deep-lined face and horny hands, standing poised at the head of his punt, with punt-pole ready for action. Bending he leans his full weight on the sturdy pole, with all the compressed vigour of the Discobolus; steadily upstream, foot by foot, he pushes and propels the punt without any disturbance of the water; oars would be useless here. On that pressure the punt hangs, held steady as a rock, while the angler delivers the cast. The novice's line falls in a horrid heap five yards from the punt, enough to frighten any fish. Paddy is ready with the cure; one deft push at the right moment, and the horrid heap straightens out, and shows the fly before the cast and line. And when the expert takes the rod, out goes the long, rippling line, and straightens just before it meets the surface downstream, well-angled; now it cuts the surface, and begins to swing round in a graceful curve, and just before it tightens a well-timed push of the pole thrills the cast, and sets a-quiver the fibres of your Silver Doctor; and the fly glints and gleams and flashes, and awakens the hunting instinct of the fish; he leaps before he looks, and his life is lost. Paddy did it. Paddy was the artist; and often the angler never knows.

Now meet Michael. Michael fishes the lake, and he has not the specialist knowledge of salmon that river gillies have. He knows a good deal about them, of course; for he catches a few every year in the lake; but salmon take time to reach his lake, and their ways are not so easily observed there, as they are in the river. Michael's speciality is the brown trout; he has studied the species for sixty years. A highly competent gillie, Michael is also a very interesting man. He is a shrewd farmer and a good judge of livestock. He has reared a family, has improved his small-holding, and now in the evening of life he gillies more for pleasure than for pay. He is a man of medium height and stocky build; and in spite of his years and occasional twinges of rheumatism, he is still as strong as a horse. He has an open cast of countenance, a firm chin, intelligent, thoughtful eyes, and the hoary head, which, says the Good Book, is "a crown of glory".*

We have fished together in sunshine and in rain for a quarter of a century, and have discussed everything under the sun, except religion. On Fridays the lunch-basket has hard-boiled eggs for him, and cold chops for me; and that is that. It is the silence of mutual respect, not indifference. We are not propagandists; and discussed religion is almost a contradiction in terms. The word *religion* comes from the Latin *religio*, a bond or tie; and if you discuss your religion much, at any rate casually, it soon ceases to be what it should be, namely a corporate bond and a personal tie.

* Proverbs xvi, 31.

Michael has no claim to College learning; but no one would dream of calling him unlearned. In many departments of knowledge he puts the College don in 'the halfpenny place'. He is an all-round craftsman and as well a natural philosopher, self-taught;* for he looks below the surface of life; he asks the *reason why*; and the term *cause* is often on his lips. He fishes and thinks. He plays the fiddle, and keeps the village conversaziones gay. He plays a good game of draughts. You cannot be long in his company without realizing that Michael has an educated mind.

What is education? In what does it essentially consist? Education includes schooling, but is a wider thing. Schooling covers 'the three *r*'s', reading, writing and arithmetic, which are the groundwork of all education; for they train the mind to use the primary symbols, letters and figures. Michael has had that training, and he is at home in both letters and figures. He counts with ease, and can reckon the price of a bullock from its weight. He reads with ease and appreciation; and if he writes with less than ease, that is because in country life the tongue largely takes the place of the pen. Michael's tongue is 'the pen of a ready writer'. His talk is almost always interesting, often instructive, and at times memorable. He is never at a loss for words, and he often puts 'the proper word in the proper place'. He likes some poetry; he can repeat the *Ancient Mariner*, and he dwells with particular appreciation upon the lines:

As idle as a painted ship
  Upon a painted ocean.

Reproductions of the ancient vellum manuscripts of Ireland, the Book of Durrow and the Book of Kells, thrill him; these marvels of calligraphy were the work of men of his race long ago. He reads widely and with enjoyment. The recent arrival of electricity in his village is a boon beyond price to him; the magic current has extinguished the flickering

* The *Philosophus autodidactus*, beloved of Arabian thinkers.

candle and the smoky paraffin lamp, and has banished the frustration of long winter evenings, dim, dreary and unprofitable. He reads the daily paper to the last line, skimming the politics. He reads fishing magazines and books on fishing. He will discuss Wood on the greased line, and can argue the case *pro* and *con*. On the whole he is against it; whatever its successes in low, clear water may be, any fish that took the surface fly in the full-flowing peaty waters of the west would, he thinks, have taken it sunk.

Books of travel and records of hazardous voyages are his chief delight; his son is named Brendan after the patron saint of voyagers. He himself has not been further afield than Scotland, where he dug coal in his early manhood without much relish for the job. He has travelled far in fancy. In his youth there lived in the village a retired sailor who had rounded Cape Horn. The Cape and sailing ships gripped his imagination; partly from that sailor and partly from books he learned much about the mysteries of sailing. He understands tacking and reefing and the use of the jib. He has never sailed; but put him aboard a sailing ship, and he would sail her. A retired Admiral kept a yacht at the Pontoon end of Lough Conn; and when she raced down the lake in a steady breeze with full canvas, she was a grand sight. Michael feasted his eyes on her, and even fishing went by the board. He has a similar feeling for the lines of a well-built boat. He has never built a boat; but he knows how they are built, and has repaired many. He can fit a new keel-band; and if you have struck a rock and holed a board, he will cut and steam and mould a new one, and leave the boat as strong and staunch as ever.

In an Irish village 'Do it yourself' is the standing order of the day; and from their youth up villagers learn to do for themselves things that town-dwellers leave to the tradesman or specialist. Even by village standards Michael's range is exceptional; he can repair almost anything from a boat to a pair of boots, from a lawn-mower to a broken fishing-rod. He has made and fitted a new stock for a hammerless gun, and he has made a fishing-rod of greenheart wood. He is no 'jack-of-all-trades'; for he knows his limits; a split-cane rod he would not attempt to build, and motor engines he leaves severely alone. There is little he does not know about the construction of a house; give him the material and time, and he will build you a house, and thatch or slate it. He does fine work, too, in metal, in wood, in fur and feather. He ties his own flies and shapes his own baits, and good flies and baits they are. The most intricate reel has no terrors for him; he will dismantle, adjust, repair and reassemble it. He understands the delicate mechanism of a watch or clock; he takes them to pieces, repairs or replaces damaged parts, and fits them together again as good as new. This skill is perhaps the climax of practical education. When strong hands that drive the stubborn plough and pull the labouring oar can handle delicate parts and adjust minute screws and tiny springs, it is sheer nonsense for educationalists to depreciate those skills, lump them together, and brand them as 'manual work', and contrast them with education and the work of mind. We may have to change our views on education and even to modify our notion of the 'mind'; but certain it is that you cannot educate hands and fingers and thumbs, as Michael's were educated, without *eo ipso* educating the mind that moves them.

These considerations are not a surrender of the case for higher education; they are a plea for a liberal approach to it. College education undoubtedly can give to many minds a pearl of great price that no manual skills and general intelligence and general reading by themselves can give. That pearl is, perhaps, detachment, detachment from the present day, detachment from the pressure of the moment. The limitations of village life and outlook no one will deny, and the chief thing missing (from the educationalist point of view) is retrospect, or an ordered sense of past time. For most folk the outside limit of their personal retrospect is 'grandfather's day'; and what happened before that is a jumble of tradition and legend. Historical studies give an ordered sense of past time; literature gives it; but nothing gives it more surely or in greater fullness than a classical education along liberal lines; for the study of the classics, raised above grammarian level, is a study of the richest periods of history and the finest literature and art. An acquaintance with the great civilizations of long ago that have moulded our law and language, our standards and institutions, gives a man a standpoint of his own, detached from the pressure of the present, from which he can observe and judge his own day and times. In the English countryside medieval cathedrals, Tudor mansions and market-places help to keep the past alive; in Ireland a few districts have their slender Round Towers to tell of the Viking invasions, and from an earlier period great monastic settlements, now in ruins, such as Clonmacnoise, the Seven Churches, and Monasterboice; but in the great majority of Irish villages there are hardly any visible links with the distant past; and to the average dweller in the west the landing of the French in Killala Bay, the Big Wind, the Potato Famine, Noah's Flood and other echoes of the sacred narrative constitute the story of the past in its effective bearing on the present day.

Let me round off the picture of my friend with a true story of a storm on the lake. This is an aspect of a gillie's life that fair-weather anglers and river anglers do not see. We learn to appreciate our gillies, when we realize that their job has its dangers that form character, and display it.

Few gillies can swim, and on the whole it is better so; the non-swimmer will not let himself be caught, if he can help it, in a situation that calls for swimming; he will not expose himself or you to danger; he trusts his boat, and he means to stay in it till he reaches land. Water is his friend and ally, not an enemy; when he is water-borne, he is in his element; he has been at the job since boyhood; it is second nature to him to do the right thing in a crisis; he understands wind and wave, and the way of a small boat in a big storm; he would not be there with you if there were any real danger. Given a good boat, two pairs of strong oars, resolute arms, stout hearts and cool heads, anglers on the western lakes will make shelter, even if they cannot reach all at once "the haven where they would be".

Courage and coolness are great qualities in a gillie, and you do not really know your man till you have been with him in a storm. Nothing tests a man like danger to life. I knew a boatman on Lough Mask who went as white as a sheet when a stiff nor'wester blew down Mountrasna Bay, and the waves were topped with white. It was no place for him, and he was not typical. Most gillies have cool heads and hearts of oak. They must have these qualities; to be cool and courageous is part of their job. Anglers want fish, and are often willing to take a chance. Whatever precautions are taken, you may be caught at a disadvantage. Storms arise suddenly; winds swing round, and plans "go all a'gley". When that happens, the courage required is not the active heroism of the soldier in action; but it is resolution, the ability to be calm and cool and collected. On a stormy lake there is little one cån *do*; man cannot pit his puny strength against wind and wave; he cannot *fight* the forces of nature; he must *use* them; and that means keeping calm and cool, and doing the right thing at the right time.

Michael and I have shared not a few anxious moments* — moments that to me were anxious; but I never once saw him flustered, much less frightened; in a tight corner he always seems to have something in reserve. His worst day on the lake is worth describing. He has often told me about it in general terms, such as, "The lake went up in smoke that day, Sir." The angler who was with him in the adventure wrote an account of it at the time, and he has shown me the record, and it is frightening still.

It was the day of an angling competition in April, 1943. The rendezvous was Coryosla Bay at the Pontoon end of Lough Conn, some eight miles by water from Cloghans, where Michael lives. It was wartime, and there was no petrol for outboard engines or for driving round by road. After breakfast Frank, a young engineer, and Michael set off in their good, solid nineteen-foot boat; it was a calm

* For an instance see below (p. 117).

morning, and Brendan, Michael's son, decided to go, too, in Michael's dinghy on the chance of a job as gillie. The dinghy was little more than a canoe, about twelve feet long, as light as a cork, with an up-turned prow at either end, like a Viking ship; it was meant for coasting about in sheltered bays in fair weather. They reached Coryosla without incident in a couple of hours; but clouds were piling up in the south; the wind was freshening; and the men knew that they were in for it. The competition gun was fired, and the anglers started work; but almost immediately the storm broke, and very soon fishing was out of the question. Lashed by wind and rain the boats ran for the nearest shelter, and tied up; anglers and gillies took refuge in hospitable cottages, where they found a welcome, warmth and tea. All the afternoon the storm raged, but lulled off about 6 p.m. Then Frank, Michael and Brendan forgathered at Coryosla and held a council of war. The issue was simple — eight easy-looking miles by water, or a trudge of twice that distance on a rough and stony road, with the prospect of returning on the morrow for boats and gear. The wind was still strong, but southerly; it should be with them all the way; rowing would be easy, and if all went well, they would be safe and sound at home within an hour and a half. That is better than a four hours' trudge, is it not? The *ayes* have it. They decided that all three should go in the big boat, and take the dinghy in tow.

For a while they were in sheltered water, and all went well; but as they drew out into the open lake, the wave was longer, and the dinghy began to misbehave. Towing is never easy in a wave; in a high and following wave it is almost impossible. Now the light dinghy would overrun and bump; now it would act as a sail and confuse the steering. To weight it and control it Michael volunteered to enter the towed dinghy and guide it with an oar. He did so, and found that he could guide it up to a point, but not control it; for as the wave grew steeper, the dinghy would poise like a surf-board on the white crest of a breaking wave, and then come sliding down the forward slope and crash against the boat. It was a terrible position for them all. Frank and Brendan shouted to Michael to come back into the comparative safety of the boat and cut the dinghy adrift. He would not hear of it; he stayed in the dinghy, cut the tow rope, and pulled clear. It was a high act of cool and calculated courage. The two men were in a solid boat with a good keel and considerable freeboard, and if they shipped a sea, the one could bale, while the other rowed; but Michael was alone in a cockle-shell, alone in the middle of an angry lake; his craft had little or no freeboard; it could spin round at a touch, and if it met a breaker broadside on, it would swamp instantaneously. But Michael never relaxed for a moment; he kept his head, and, watching every wave like a lynx, by sheer boatcraft he remained in full control of his frail barque.

An hour passed, and now in the gathering gloom the following wind had brought boat and dinghy to a point within half a mile of Rinmore Point, and if they could round that headland, there lay safety and a lee shore. Suddenly the wind failed them, and veered; the south wind that had blown all day dropped, and there was for a few moments an oily calm, an ominous calm, more fearsome than the storm; away to the west, high up in the sky over the shoulder of Mount Nephin, appeared the lurid red glow that told of a change of wind and of a hurricane on the way. They pulled frantically; for they were abreast the long, pitiless Brackwanshagh Reef. The last few yards made all the difference. They had just cleared the reef, and had entered Storm Bay,* when they heard a rumble; and with a roar like an express train a tornado from the west struck the lake. Then (in the words of Frank's record) "the squall hit us in a cloud of spray. It enveloped us completely and sent us hurtling towards the shore. All I could do was to keep our stern square to the wind. I kicked my rubber boots off. Soon the boat was travelling at such speed that I feared she would split in two when the crash came. A thole-pin broke, and I lost the last vestige of control. Suddenly Brendan started;

* The name 'Storm Bay' commemorates this adventure.

he saw the line of white breakers ahead. I felt the keel grating on the rocks. Then a great wave took us up and hurled us broadside-on right over the rocks and into the sandy pool beyond. Twenty yards away we could dimly see Michael calmly tying up his tiny dinghy."

CHAPTER VIII

THE WESTERN LAKES

THE large lakes of Counties Mayo and Galway are, from north to south, Conn, Mask and Corrib. There is good angling for trout on all three; and if this chapter centres on Lough Conn, that is because I happen to know it best. I have fished Corrib occasionally. The western shores of Mask I know quite well; Conn I have fished for thirty years. The three lakes, from the angler's point of view, have the same general character, and what is said of one of them applies in large measure to the others also. On the map the three lakes look like a chain; they may have a common geological origin, and they have several features in common. They are limestone lakes, and the trout in them are of fine quality; they are lusty, deep-shouldered, pink-fleshed like salmon, and they run a good size. Every now and then one meets an outsize trout, such as the one described below (p. 130). The wet-fly fishing for trout is much the same on all three lakes. The dapping season is better defined on Corrib and on Mask, and visitors go there to dap the mayfly. On Conn the hatch of mayfly is long-drawn-out, but never heavy; once it begins there will be a small hatch every day through June, July and August, and even in September; one takes a few fish with the artificial mayfly; but there is never much of the natural fly on the water at one time; and the dapping on Conn is mostly with the harry-long-legs (the 'daddy') and the grasshopper. There are salmon and grilse in Conn and Corrib, and they take both fly and bait. Any migrants that reach Mask must pass through the long underground river between Mask and Corrib, and few fish make it. That shapely and beautifully coloured little fish, the char,* is occasionally taken in Conn. Coarse fish, pike and perch, are to be had in all three lakes. That curious variety of brown trout, the gillaroo,† the trout with a gizzard, is often taken in Mask, but never, I think, in Conn.

The Inland Fisheries Trust, a body set up in 1951 by the Government, has been making valiant efforts in recent years to improve the angling on these lakes. The general impression is that these lakes 'went off' catastrophically some twenty or more years ago. There is evidence to support this view; but conclusive statistics are hard to come by; and one must make allowance for the vagaries of angling memory. We remember the good days and forget the bad; our own angling 'goes off', and we say the lake 'has gone off'; we grow old and cannot fish as hard as we did, and we blame the lake for our smaller catches. Various causes modify and change the feeding habits of trout; there may be as many as ever in the lake, though fewer respond to our flies and baits.

In this case, however, the pessimists are probably right. The lakes do seem to yield less than they did, whatever the reason. In 1927 or 1928 an angler fished Mask for the month of August, less Sundays, and took one hundred trout, averaging two pounds in weight. That would work out at well over four fish, four good fish, a day. With that figure in mind consider the following figures taken from the official records of a qualifying competition in trout-angling, open to the world, held on Mask on 8 and 9 June, 1957. On 8 June, 87 rods competed; total catch, 70 trout. On 9 June, 94 rods competed; total catch, 56 trout. The individual catches of those who qualified for the Final were:

* See below (p. 146). † Irish for 'red fellow'.

8 June			9 June		
Fish	*Weight*		*Fish*	*Weight*	
	lb.	oz.		lb.	oz.
5	5	5	2	4	10¼
7	4	¼	3	3	10¾
2	3	11¾	1	2	11
3	3	9	3	2	10
2	2	5½	1	2	7
3	3	4½	2	2	2¾
3	2	11	2	2	1
2	2	5	2	2	
1	2	2	2	1	12
2	2	1¼	2	1	11

These results are disappointing. Anglers of experience fished all day at a good season of the year, when trout should have been stirring to the mayfly, and some of them caught nothing, and no one made a good catch. It seems a poor return for the work and money the Trust has put into the rehabilitation of these lakes.

Are these results typical? Competitions are notoriously unlucky in the weather. What does local opinion say? Do local anglers consider that the measures taken by the Inland Fisheries Trust are meeting with success? On Lough Conn local opinion is divided. Some anglers have done better in the last year or two, and some have not; some praise the work of the Trust, and some do not; some think that the fishing is definitely on the upgrade; some think that the decline has but been arrested, and others even take the pessimistic view that the angling is worse than it was. Personally I think it too early for a final judgment. The improvement on Conn — if by 'improvement' be meant an increase in the number and weight of trout taken by anglers — is slight, and far from commensurate with the time and money expended by the Trust. What some anglers put down to an improvement in the angling may be really an improvement in the outboard engine. Twenty years ago we spent hours pulling the cord in vain; and if we did get the engine started, we dared not run it slow, or it would cut out. Now the outboard has about reached perfection; a flick, and in a minute or two we are at the head of the drift, ready for work. We can get much more angling in a much shorter time than formerly. Then, too, the improvement in the outboard has meant a vast increase in the amount of trolling; and angling clubs may have to consider the question seriously in years to come. I say nothing against an occasional bit of trolling when you want a trout for supper, and cannot get it in a more sporting way; but there are duffers who spend literally the livelong day in chug-chugging round the lake with two spoons out and a team of flies; and they sometimes get big bags, especially in March and April. The figures get round, and get into the papers, and give a rather misleading impression about the improvement in angling proper.

Trolling apart, however, some sporting anglers who use nothing but the fly-rod have done better in recent years; but they are mostly anglers on the spot who have farms to work and therefore choose their fishing days with great care, and do get better results. On the other hand those anglers who are on holiday, and fish the lake day after day, no matter what the weather, do not take the rosy view. They may get more fish than formerly when the weather conditions are perfect; under poor conditions they may get less. If there is a squally cloud, like a man's hand, on the horizon, you may fish the best drifts in Lough Conn hour after hour, with a fine breeze and good clear light, and get absolutely no response. "What has the Trust done?" you say to yourself. "There's not a fish in the lake."

On the whole I incline to the opinion that there are rather more trout in Lough Conn as the result of the work of the Trust than there were ten years ago; but that they do not rise to the fly as freely as they did twenty years ago.* The trout are stiffer than they were, because they are in better form and are better fed, and do not need to take chances. The principal activity of the Trust has been the removal of

* See the family records given below (p. 121) for 1940-6.

perch; scores of perch traps have been moored in the bays for the past few years, and perch have been removed by the ton. There are many left; and anglers catch almost as many as ever on trolls and flies; and the total elimination of pests and predators from these large lakes is an idle dream; still, their numbers have been greatly reduced, and that ought to mean more trout; for perch eat greedily, and are partial to trout fry and trout eggs.* The increase in the trout population is not necessarily passed on to the angler, for the first few years at any rate; for fewer perch means more bottom feeding for the trout, and that means fat, bottom-feeding, contented trout, who will not rise to the surface and take your fly, unless angling conditions are exceptionally favourable; and that is my tentative diagnosis of the present condition of Conn.

One thing is certain: the trout are there; the trout are there, in Conn and Mask and Corrib, and there in sufficient numbers and quality to make angling for them well worthwhile almost any day from March to September, inclusive. And there is always the chance of an exceptionally large fish and exceptionally large numbers. Here are some assorted facts and figures. Mr. Joseph Adams, a clergyman, in his *The Angler's Guide to the Irish Fisheries*, London, n.d. (*c.* 1930), describes a day on Conn on which they took 17 lb. weight of trout before lunch (p. 146). In his later book *Fifty Years Angling* (p. 209) he says that the fishing in Conn is not "as good as it used to be". Mr. James Kelly of Cloghans took 45 trout on a June day some twenty years ago; on that same day Mr. Michael Clarke of Cloghans was out with a novice, and they took 20 trout, and lost many. Mr. Clarke has fished Conn for sixty years, and his largest catch, to date, is 24 trout (September). My own largest catch for a day on Conn is 19 trout (July). On 8 September, 1957, Mr. Martin Kelly took 17 trout with the fly, fishing up and down all day from Rinmore Point to Sandy Bay with an offshore wind.†

* Trout retaliate, of course, and take perch fry greedily; and when they are on the perch fry, they will not look at your fly unless it be a Butcher on the tail, which is no bad imitation of the silvery fry.

† N.B. In all these cases the catch given is the boat catch, usually two rods.

Numbers and size are attractions to any angler worth his salt; but the beauty of the trout in these limestone lakes, their colouring, their trim, tense shape and potential strength, are perhaps greater attractions. Once you have seen a ten-pound trout, with golden belly and both flanks patterned with red spots and black, come flashing out of the water in a head and tail rise at your bob-fly, arched like the bow of Ulysses, you never forget the sight; and if you have ever sat in a boat on a lake for two hours and a half while your companion played a dynamic trout of that weight and more, you will be wedded to that lake for life.

Lough Conn is said to mean 'the Lake of the Hound', taking its name from the Irish word *cu*, a dog. Its shape on the map, with fancy's help, can be viewed as the outline of a dog. The winner of the Grand National some years ago, sportsmen will remember, bore the name Lough Conn. The tough little winner of that testing chase was born and bred beside the lake, and pulled the plough there in sight of anglers. The lake lies nearly due north and south. From Gortnaraby at the northern end, not far from Crossmolina, to Pontoon Bridge at the southern end is almost eight miles as the crow flies. From Cloghans Bay on the eastern side to the gaunt ruins of Errew Hotel* on the western edge of the lake is some two miles and a half. The perimeter of the lake is much longer, and its full extent much greater than these measurements would suggest. The lake is festooned with long creeks and wide bays; there are creeks and bays to suit every wind that blows — a great comfort to the angler. To coast round the lake, taking in all its inlets and indentations would be a big undertaking; we might reckon it as thirty miles or more.

The lake is dominated by Nephin, a lone mountain 2,640 feet high, on its western shores. The weather-wise angler always keeps a weather eye on Nephin; it is a barometer in which he reads the pressure, watching the cloud layers moving up and down, and in the clarity, or otherwise, of its

* Accidentally burnt some years ago. The masonry looks as strong as ever; it resembles that of Mount Falcon, Ballina.

contour a good deal can often be read as to the feelings of the fish and the prospects for the day. Nephin has a volcanic appearance; it is well worth climbing, and is a safe climb from Lahardaun, provided always that the mountain top is free from cloud, and that there is no prospect of mist or fog for the next three hours and a half — the time it takes to go up and down. Lough Mask, Lough Corrib, and Clew Bay are well seen from the summit on a clear day, and Lough Conn with all its creeks and bays and islands lies like a map at your feet. Nephin is the sister mountain to Croagh Patrick. They are of almost identical height, Nephin, I am told, being a few feet higher. They are alike in general appearance. Croagh Patrick, as all Irishmen know, is the height from which St. Patrick banished from his island snakes and toads and other evil things. Croagh Patrick, crowned with its chapel, is in full view to the south-west and west from most parts of the northern end of Conn; and if the wind sits in that quarter, keep your eye on Croagh Patrick; it will tell you what weather is coming.

Lough Conn narrows towards its centre; from Chain Island* on the west to Rinmore Point on the east is not much more than half a mile; and a long half-mile it is when you must make the crossing on a stormy day. The sou'west wind is whistling round the point of Chain, and eastward bound your little boat sets out for the shelter of Rinmore. Longer and longer grows the wave, and higher and higher its crest as you approach Rinmore, and as you round the point into safety, beware of the last angry breaker, usually on the watch there, as if disappointed and chagrined at your escape.

A gillie and a good boat are essential to safe angling on the western lakes. Conn is no more dangerous than the others; they must all *always* be treated with respect. The gillies at Tourmakeady on the western shores of Mask rarely meet their opposite numbers from Ballinrobe on the eastern shores, though the distance is not great. "You never know,"

* Chain Island, so called, is the southern point of the peninsula on which stand the ruins of the abbey or friary of Errew. Another monastic foundation, Derry or Derragh, which is perpetuated in the name Derramore, is mentioned in the *Annals of Clonmacnoise*, *sub anno* 1404.

one of them said to me in sepulchral tones, "you never know what's coming over thon hill." You push off in a mill-pond surface, and start up the engine, and in five minutes the mill-pond surface may become a raging sea.

> In gallant trim the gilded vessel goes
>   Youth on the prow, and Pleasure at the helm;
> Regardless of the sweeping whirlwind's sway.*

A boat twenty-one feet long and about five feet seven inches in the beam will ride a rough lake, and will fish it well, rough or smooth. Those dimensions allow five thwarts or seats, and will take in comfort two, three, or four people, and more on a calm day. It can be driven safely, if slowly, by an outboard engine in a high wind, short of a storm or gale, and without an engine two pairs of oars in capable hands can manage it under all reasonable conditions. In a light breeze one pair of sculls can row it with ease. A good deep keel, well bound, is all-important. The stern or transom should be strengthened with double stays to take the weight and vibration of the engine, and should be inspected regularly for any signs of 'give'; for that is where boating tragedies begin. The bow should be covered so as to form a cubby hole with a door; for here inside you will keep the lunch basket and anything that cannot stand splash and spray and rain; and on the outside you will sit when casting, unless the wave is high; it makes a grand raised seat, commanding the water well, and puts the finishing touch to a well-found angling boat.

Oars and oarage need attention; the outboard engine has nearly reached perfection; still she may refuse, especially in a cold March and April; and sometimes in a rough sea or in the shallows or near the rocks you dare not start her up. Always have two pair of oars aboard, long oars for the centre seat, sculls for the bow. Iron rowlocks are a snare and a delusion; they drop overboard, and leave you nicely stuck; or the oars slip through them when you are playing a fish.

* Thomas Gray (1716-71), *The Bard.*

Pegs are far better; wooden pegs, even if made of heart of oak, break when the strain comes — and there is a terrific strain when wind and wave are against you. Iron pegs are the only thing. Wedge them firmly in their holes; and have a strong wooden bracket, covered with leather, fixed to the oar and pivoting on the peg. The oars will then look after themselves, leaving your hands free to attend to the rod or the net.

The gillie should know the lake like the palm of his hand; and most of them do so; but one day a Lough Mask gillie was taking me out, and boasting of his prowess, "And I know every rock in the lake, Sir." As he said the word, Crash! Bang!; we hit a rock. "An' that's one of 'em," cried Paddy, with superb *aplomb*. He must know the lake at every height of water; a three-inch rise or fall makes it a new lake; the rocks that were danger-points are so no longer, and new dangers take their place.

Castle Bay near Cloghans is a fine sheltered haven for Lough Conn boats (though the Home Bay is better); but no stranger could possibly bring his boat in and out without a gillie. At normal summer level the entrance to Castle Bay is guarded by a veritable Scylla and Charybdis. Scylla is a rock, named Sally, usually a foot or so below the surface in summertime. Charybdis is a broad shallow, a fine fishing ground, but inhospitable to boats. Between these two perils there is a deep gut where salmon lie in springtime. The gut is some 50 yards wide, but it only offers some 35 yards of effective sea-room. This gut runs diagonally across the mouth of Castle Bay, and is the only way in and out. It is easy to find if you know the landmarks; without that knowledge it cannot be done. In calm water a boat might bump its way in; a boat running for shelter in a storm would almost certainly be wrecked.

Those who would enjoy the delights of the western lakes must be alive to their dangers. And so a word about storms.* A real storm is no danger to the wise angler; for he is not caught out in it. It is useless to fish in a storm, or when a

* See also above (pp. 104ff).

storm is imminent. The danger comes from 'the half and half' storm, coupled with the lure, or as Virgil calls it, the love,* of the further shore. The wise angler watches the barometer, listens to the forecasts, reads the local signs, and if there is a storm brewing, he does not go out, or if he does go out, he does not go far from home; he goes upwind, and he keeps to his own side of the lake. There are gales in which no small craft could live, when, in Michael's phrase, "the lake goes up in smoke". In such a storm one must make for the nearest shelter, haul the boat up, and wait, or walk home. The real danger comes from the 'half and half' storm when one is caught on the far side of the lake. The 'walk home' might be twenty miles; the 'wait' might be twenty-four hours; by crossing the open lake one can be home in ten minutes or so, and one is tempted to take a chance.

When you stand on the far shore, and look across the stormy lake to the haven where you would be, you know where you are, *if the wind is against you*; for the biggest breakers are breaking at your feet. If the wind is with you, the biggest breakers are waiting for you on the far side, and how big will they be? That is the question.

"Well, Michael, what'll we do? The west wind is strong and freshening; here we are on the western shore at the old Abbey, and yonder across the lake is Castle Bay. The white horses are out. Can we make it?" Michael looks back at Nephin, and then scans the waste of waters, and reads all the signs, and replies, "Yes, Sir, we'll make it all right. It'll be a rough crossing, but we'll get there."

Flick, flick, goes the starting-cord, and we are off; with the strong following wind we are soon gathering speed, ten, fifteen, twenty miles an hour. At first it is grand, effortless like flying. Soon we are in the open, near the middle of the lake. Then comes the warning. A sudden qualm; the boat slithers; steering is confused; side waves splash into the boat; white combers are ahead, and astern is a moving wall

* *Aeneid*, VI, 314: "*ripae ulterioris amore*". Haunted words, too poignant perhaps for this light-hearted application.

of water that looks as if it might fall on us and poop us. It is a warning; we are travelling too fast; there is no thought of turning back; turn off the engine, and tilt it up; shut off the oil; have the baler ready; say a silent prayer, and leave the rest to Michael. There he is up in the bow in full control, sculls in hand. In a very high wind he will turn the bow upwind and back the boat downwind; but there is no need for that today. He goes straight on downwind, tipping the wave now left, now right, to keep her straight. No pulling is required; wind and wave do it all. It is as thrilling as a switchback in a circus. There's Michael in the bow up on the crest of a wave, smiling down at you, like Olympian Jove. Now he is down in the trough, and you are up on the crest, and when you are really up, you could fancy you see beneath you to the bottom of the lake. Now we are nearing harbour, feeling the full force of wind and wave. We are at the entrance to Castle Bay; but Scylla and Charybdis lie between us and safety. No need for landmarks today. There stands angry Sally with the white foam and surge swirling and hissing all around her; we swish past her five yards off; a few deft strokes of the right oar, and we are in the gut clear of the shallows; wind and wave have lost their terrors; we are on an even keel in Castle Bay, and are soon safe and sound on dry land.

And now a word about engine-craft and boat-craft; for there is more to learn about the western lakes than the art of catching fish in them. When running the engine between the drifts in a moderate wave, drive straight into the wave, as far as possible; it is safest and driest, and keeps the boat steady in its whole length, and there is little or no splash. If the wave is heavy, slow down. Driven fast against a high wave, the boat rears up like a mettled horse, and the bow comes crashing down, shivering the timbers and opening the seams, and the bow thwart will break if a heavy weight is on it. Run slow, but not too slow, lest the engine stall. A following wind is heady, like champagne, and, like it, calls for care. The boat is soon running at twenty miles per hour, and when the wave gets long and steep, the boat may side-slip on the crest and slither down the slope. Slow down at once. Side winds are a special study. Usually one can drive with safety down the long furrow with a wall of water on either side; but watch the crest of the wave, and if it looks like breaking, take no chance; go slow. A side wave can sometimes be negotiated in corkscrew fashion, like a crab. There is a big wave a-beam that looks threatening; sidestep into it; the boat will rise to it; then straighten out again into the long furrow, till the next big one comes along; then repeat the manœuvre. The ancient Greeks thought that every third wave was the big one, and they gave it a name; on the western lakes the rhythm of the big wave is nearer one in seven than one in three.

Head wind, side wind and following wind — each one has its thrills and its dangers. Experience soon teaches how to deal with them. Boats are built to float, and provided your boat is seaworthy, broad in the beam, with a good deep keel, and provided the helmsman keeps cool and the children do not stand up or panic, all will be well. The worst situation to meet is the huddle of waters; you meet it rounding a point on a gusty day; wind and wave come at you on both sides all at once; and you have hardly time to think or take your bearings; in such a case shut off the engine at once, and leave it to the gillie. Boats are made to float, and they do float; they right themselves in a wonderful way, provided they are given time, and are not forced at speed.

And now for boat-craft. Boat-craft proper is much more than pulling an oar or a pair of oars; it is managing the boat like an artist or craftsman; it involves a certain oneness between boat and boatman; for he must express himself, his intentions and purpose, in the movements of his boat. King Solomon found three things too wonderful for him, yea four which he knew not* — and one of the four was the way of a ship in the midst of the sea. Watch the bow of the violin in the hand of the *maestro*, or the fingers of the organist on the keys of the cathedral organ, and watch the oars in Michael's

* Proverbs xxx, 18, 19.

hands. King Solomon had seen his proud ship of Tarshish in full sail with its cargo of ivory, of apes and peacocks; and a gallant sight it was. Michael's way with his boat on a drift on Lough Conn is a thing of wonder, too.

Gillies do not pull a very strong oar, as a rule; they eat so little meat, and their technique in pulling is not what it might be. The College student in his old school tie or boatclub tie, down for the fishing, will beat the gillie in the boat race at the local regatta; but the gillie has what the student cannot have, boat-craft. The gillie is one with his boat; he is born to it; in action his two oars are extensions of his two arms; to see what should be done, and to do it, with him are one and the same thing. In the tricky launching or landing, when strong winds are blowing athwart, he seems to feel the boat as a whole; he knows the exact position and angle of bow and stern and centre; he reckons sub-consciously with currents and sideblast; he feels in his bones the amount of freeboard, and the strike of the wind on bow and stern; he is one with his boat; if he shifts his seat, or bids you do so, that is the reason why.

On the drift his craft rises to the level of an art, and anglers often owe fish to the gillie's art as well as to their own. Seated towards the stern on the last thwart but one, the gillie angles the boat to the breeze, bow-in for an in-shore breeze, bow-out for an off-shore breeze. With one oar or scull out behind he is in full control; with one push in she goes; with one pull out she comes, no matter how high the wave. If you want fish on the western lakes, you must cast near the rocks, and the gillie has one eye on the look-out for the yellow gleam of wrecking rock. In a very light breeze he works sideways, like a crab; he makes the most of every flurry of air; and often it is his oar that imparts to your fly the twist or turn that gives you a trout.

So much for the general conditions of trout angling on the western lakes; in the next chapter we tell of the fishing itself.

Appendix to Chapter VIII

Trout taken on Lough Conn, 1940-6 — one boat, two to three rods. 'Spring' means April; 'Summer' means July, August or early September.

	Spring			*Summer*		
	No. of days fished	*Total No. of trout taken*	*Average weight*	*No. of days fished*	*Total No. of trout taken*	*Average weight*
1940	—	—	—	34	171	14¾ oz.
1941	9	67	16 oz.	36	206	16 oz.
1942	—	—	—	41	152	15¾ oz.
1943	7	65	15 oz.	11	26	19 oz.
1944	—	—	—	34	65	19 oz.
1945	—	—	—	28	76	22 oz.
1946	5	35	18½ oz.	26	83	15½ oz.

Best day for weight: 6 August, 1945, 5 trout, two of 4 lb. each, on the dap, three on the fly, one of 2½ lb., and two of 2 lb.

Best days for number: 9 April, 1943, 18 trout weighing 16 lb. 10 April, 1943, 11 trout weighing 11 lb. 19 July, 1940, 13 trout weighing 12 lb.

Breakdown of methods of summer catch 1941:

Total trout taken: 206 — dap 37, troll 16, wet-fly 153 (Golden Olive 36, Invicta 8, Green Olive 8, and other patterns)

CHAPTER IX

A DAY ON LOUGH CONN

IT is a gracious day in late August. How good to be alive and well! The glass is high and tending upwards. At 10 a.m. the car draws up at Michael's snug little house, built to withstand the winter's storms. Its turf fire never goes out, and this morning the blue smoke rises straight as a pillar. Through the open door come the strains of Radio Luxembourg. Beside the doorway, gripping the thatch, stand the two fly rods. Here comes Michael, a happy smile on his weather-beaten face; he cannot do heavy farm-work now; his son does it for him; but he is as good as ever at the oar and the rod; and he loves the lake and the boat and the fishing. Bruno barks his welcome, and scatters the hens, and is sent about his business. Quiet is restored, and greetings are exchanged. Then comes the important question. "What's the day going to do, Michael? There's not a breath. Look at that smoke." "Aye, Sir," replies Michael, "but look higher at those fleecy clouds; there's carry in them; there'll be plenty of breeze soon, and it should be a good day."

In the back of the car are the necessities of an angler's life — the tin of petrol, duly mixed, the volcano kettle, the teapot and lunch basket. "Put in your overalls, Michael, and don't forget the pipe; we'ld have no luck without it." Michael goes on with the rods and opens the gate for the car. The cocks and hens and turkeys and ducks and geese give way, and the old gander hisses defiance. We pass through the open gate and across the headland of a field of oats, ripening yellow, and there, the other side of the honeysuckle hedge, are the blue waters of Lough Conn, already slightly ruffled.

We are off for the day, and must check up on the *impedimenta*. Nothing must be overlooked — newspapers to boil the kettle, matches, cups, tea, sugar, and salt; it takes a deal of things to make and keep an angler happy; and *one* essential overlooked may mar the day. Waders are essential for launching and landing and protection against rain and splash; and it is sure to rain if you leave your mackintosh behind. The perfect angling kit for boat-work has yet to be devised. Oil-skin and skirt are good; thick mackintosh and thigh boots are better; but when it really rains on Lough Conn, there is no kit, known to me, will keep a man dry both *a priori* and *a posteriori*. The net should be large enough to take a grilse; a gaff is wanted for the salmon or outsize trout, see below (p. 130). India-rubber boat cushions are almost essential; Michael prefers his folded sack. Spare petrol, mixed, and a filler or tun-dish should be brought; and anglers have been known to bring everything else, and forget their rods and tackle. The fly rod should be set up, complete with reel and cast and flies, before launching.

About flies, how many do you fish? Lough Conn anglers mostly fish four. Four flies cast well, especially in a stiff breeze, and they alight as a team on the water. Besides, two places on the team are permanently filled with indispensables, and two places are needed for experiment to find 'the fly of the day'. Golden Olive and Invicta, lake size, are almost indispensable; they are, I fancy, the most widely used patterns on these lakes. You may find nature's Golden Olive in your boat almost any summer's day, and a large, handsome, juicy fly it is. The Invicta is not unlike it, and may deputize for the mayfly, too. The other Olives have their days, and should be tried, Sooty, Green and Dark Green, especially Sooty. Other flies for the experimental places are, the mayfly, Connemara Black (on the tail), Watson's Fancy, Wasp, Teal and Gold, Teal and Green, Thunder and Lightning, Jungle Cock and Silver (on the tail), Partridge and Fiery Brown. These are worth their places almost any day, the brighter ones on the brighter days. *Desperation Flies* are (if the list saddens you, reader, please pass it by, of your charity) Claret, Coch-a-bundy, Coachman, Peter Ross, Orange and Grouse, Daddy-long-legs; we put them up when we are sure there is not a fish in the lake, and they sometimes do the trick. The Grasshopper Fly is a thing of beauty, with its green flash and tinge of red; it kills in July. A dark blue fly, round like a blue-bottle, fished on the tail and well sunk, occasionally persuades; and there is a modest, inconspicious fly that would never take an angler, but does take trout — its name has slipped my memory; it has the over-all look of a March Brown, with a dab of green in the body. Michael took five good trout with it one day. I hadn't it, and couldn't stir a tail. There are two very distinct varieties of mayfly, the gaudy double-winged (for the bob) and the more sober hackle fly (for the tail); both should be tried when the green drake is on the water. The black, spent-gnat mayfly, deadly on Sheelin, does nothing on Conn. And I forgot to mention the Confidence Fly; it is perhaps the best of all; it is the 'old faithful' you trust; it may be a nameless, dowdy old veteran, but you fish well with it and keenly. You have killed with it before, and will kill with it again. Give it its chance.

In the launching, as in the landing, all chores are shared. On some waters the angler is the paying passenger, and the gillie the hired man, and the angler does nothing but fish. On Conn the 'boat spirit' rules; the boat and all the men in it are one entity, for the time being, with a common interest and a common object; therefore we share the work. For the same reason we rarely speak of 'my catch' or 'his catch', but of 'the catch', the boat's catch. If another boat hails us, and shouts, What luck? we answer with the boat's catch, not that of individual rods. The 'boat spirit' doubles the joys of lake fishing, and halves its sorrows. Sorrows abound;

frustration is always round the corner, and every little courtesy helps. A wet-fly angler from a boat makes eight or nine casts a minute. Call it ten casts for ease of calculation; at that rate there would be 600 casts an hour, and in six hours you and I make 3,600 casts apiece; and all but one or two of those piscatorial efforts go for nothing. It is no wonder we feel the frustration, and get 'fed up'. A touch of the 'boat spirit' is a magic salve to frayed tempers, especially when, as often happens, the trout come to one end of the boat and not to the other.

Launching is easy today. Michael gives the word; the props are released, a couple of shoves, and the boat is afloat. "Now, Sir, you get in." I get in and walk astern, and hold an oar to punt her off. Michael gets in, and our day on Conn has begun. The breeze is light, inclining south; it is too light to fish Castle Bay, and we decide to run upwind, and be ready for the breeze when it comes. The engine starts like a bird, and a ten minutes' run across the open brings us to Brackwanshagh Bay. The name is Irish, meaning 'the bay of the speckled trout'. It is not so much a bay, as a broad shallows, running far out into the lake; it gets every breath of air that blows, and is a happy hunting ground in a light breeze. At the head of the drift I stop the engine, tilt it up, turn off the oil, move to the bow, take up my rod, and begin the day's work. From the other end of the boat Michael with one oar out controls the drift, and when all is in trim, he too takes his rod and works away. If there is no one else to take the second rod, the gillie should fish; he enjoys doing so, as a rule; it contents him, and your chances of fish are doubled. A third fly rod is a mistake. The rod in the centre can only cast backwards and forwards; the other two rods have more latitude, but they are deprived of the 'Lough Conn flick' — a wristy, clever throw, like the Spey cast; it brings the curling cast of flies too close to the plane in which the centre rod is working. Two *fly* rods is all the boat will take in comfort; but there is room for a dapping-rod in the centre, if the lady or the youngster would like to have a go.

At Brackwanshagh point there is a pool, half an acre in

extent, walled about with submerged rocks, a famous feeding-ground for trout. On a rough day it is inaccessible; but its winding entrance can be negotiated in a light wave. Rising nothing outside in the open, we pull quietly into the pool, and my first cast takes a nice trout, a pounder — Golden Olive on the bob; without ceremony he is swung to the back of the boat, where Michael is waiting with the net. Then it was Michael's turn; he took a larger trout with an Invicta of his own tying — rather darker than usual, in some lights deadly. I netted Michael's fish. By now only some twenty yards of the pool remain unfished; but we fish it out; in a pool the best is often at the end; the nearer the bone the sweeter the meat, and the nearer the rocks the larger the trout. Michael has reeled up; for he must take the oars; he has actually begun to pull out, when my reel screams, and the top joint bends double; it is a big one, to the Connemara Black on the tail. The trout pulls; I pull; Michael pulls; the first job is to get him away from the rocks; for if he gets down amongst them, we may never be able to winkle him out. Soon we are in deep water in the centre of the pool, and all is under control. He makes a few rushes, and then tires and surfaces at the back of the boat; before he can recover, firmly applied pressure swings him over the waiting net; he is a comely fish, three pounds in weight, in the pink of condition, with tiny head, deep shoulders, and nearly as broad as long.

Three nice trout from the Pool — it is a good start. We pull out to the open and fish along the edge of the reef. The breeze is freshening from the south, and we drift at a smart pace. One or two fish boil up at the fly, but do not take. Soon we come to the point of Storm Bay, where some years ago Michael in his 12-foot dinghy was caught by a sudden westerly gale and was swept ashore over a surging wall of rock.* At the point there is usually a feeding fish, and he did not fail us today. Just round the point, too, in the calm is always worth a try; my Connemara Black was lying there in the still water a lifeless lump of feathers; a small fresh-run

* See above (p. 106).

salmon took it, and paid the penalty. A brief midday rise gave us two more trout, and then everything went slack. I looked at my watch — it was 1.30 p.m. "Are you hungry, Michael?" "Well, Sir, the fish aren't; shall we land and have lunch?"

If the day is not too hot or too cold or breezy, a picnic lunch on the shores of Conn, or one of its islands, is a pleasant affair. The landing-place must be chosen with care. An exposed shore must be avoided, no matter how light the breeze; even a small wave will rock the boat against the stones, and her timbers will suffer. A quiet sandy bay is best; second-best is the lee side of a headland. Draw the boat well up out of the reach of wave or backwash, and make allowance for sudden squalls. The boat will be forgotten during the lunch-hour; before you start to prepare the lunch make sure that the boat is in a fit state to be forgotten; or you may wake up from your *siesta* to see your good ship floating out to sea and to find yourself marooned.

Lough Conn water makes excellent tea. A volcano camp kettle and two or three newspapers will boil enough water in five minutes for four or five people. If you are a tea-drinker, and not in a hurry, and would like an angler's lunch fit for a king, make a fire of wood; there is dry drift-wood on most shores, or dead furze, or, best of all, dead ivy. Make a good big fire, and while the kettle is boiling, get the gillie to clean a couple of small trout, under the pound, if you have any such; wrap them securely in folds of news-paper; soak them well in water; lay them amid the wood embers that are still glowing; turn them two or three times; and in ten minutes there is a fish course, the envy of epicures, Conn trout broiled, piping hot.

Young folk bundle into their boats the moment lunch is over, and there is some excuse for haste if the morning has been bad and the afternoon has turned propitious. On the day I am describing we did not hurry away after lunch; we were well satisfied with our morning's work; the early afternoon is not the best time of day for a trout; and the gillie deserves more consideration than he sometimes gets.

He is 'on the go' and on the watch all the time we are afloat, and, especially if he is no longer young, he likes a leisurely lunch, followed by a leisurely pipe and a story or two, and a short snooze; there is a bit of washing up to be done; the boat may need teeming, if the season has been hot and dry; and there are always casts to be examined and tested, and flies to be changed.

Soon after half-past three we were afloat again. The breeze held steady from the south; the sun was playing hide and seek with light, fleecy clouds; the air was clear, and expectation rose; we engined upwind, and it was on four o'clock when we reached the head of the drift. Whether it is the cool of the day coming on, or the slope of the sun's rays, or just the regular habits of our finny ancestors, I do not know; but there is no doubt that '4 p.m.' is the witching hour on Lough Conn in July and August and early September. We count on the four o'clock rise; nor did it fail us this day. We had drifted the same water in the morning, had taken fish in pet spots, but there had been nothing like a general rise; in the afternoon the whole stretch was alive; from four o'clock to six we counted some forty rises; they were not taking very well, but we netted eight nice* trout, making thirteen trout and one salmon for the day.

A change came over the day soon after six, and we understood then why we had not done better; the wind veered to the sou'west, and blew up and took on a cold edge; the air turned smoky; clouds piled up in the southern sky; the sun retired for the day, and there was every prospect of a wet and stormy night. "All over for the day, Michael?" "Yes, Sir; it's time to reel up and go." Just to warm up I took the oars, and pulled for ten minutes downwind, while Michael let out the trolls; but it was no good; when a change in the day puts the trout off the fly, it usually puts them off the bait as well. Pike and perch are not so choosy, and we took one of each variety as we rounded Rinmore Point. Starting up the

* A 'nice trout' in local parlance, or 'a nice shtump of a trout' means a trout weighing between one pound and two and a half pounds; anything heavier is individualized; anything lighter would be a 'keeper' or a 'throw-back'.

engine we were soon speeding across the open with following wind and wave; by the time we reached our bay the white horses were out; but we were soon in the shelter; at our little haven we placed the runners with care and drew the good boat high and dry, with one more pull for luck; the four props are firmly fixed, and keep her rigid fore and aft; the engine is covered against the rain; and for fear of a nor'west gale a chain is passed round a thwart and tied to a boulder on one side of the boat, and on the other side a couple of old car tyres are wedged in to serve as bumpers. Man can do no more; it will be a dirty night; but the lake is not rising, and all is secure with a margin to spare. Back we go to the cottage and the car. Thirteen trout and a salmon — it is nothing to brag about; but we have often done worse; and we say good-night, well pleased with Lough Conn and our catch.

Before we leave Lough Conn let me tell of another day there with a trout of exceptional size as the central theme. For the benefit of those who are not familiar with the limestone lakes, and who may be sceptical about the size and weight of the trout in them, I will introduce the theme with a curtain-raiser about a Lough Mask trout. Here is an extract from the *Irish Times* for the 18 June, 1957: "A trout weighing 13 lb. 2 oz. was landed by Mr. R. G. Syme of Coolnastud, Gorey, on Saturday from Lough Mask at Ballinrobe. It was the eleventh largest trout* to be taken

* 'Eleventh largest' appears to be a reference to the list of large trout contained in the *Angler's Guide to the Irish Free State*, 3rd ed., Dublin, 1937, pp. 204ff. The fifth edition (1957) of that work has cut out the greater part of that list for reasons of space, but it has made amends by a very interesting note (ibid., p. 224) on 'Pepper's Ghost'. It tells us that the stuffed fish is extant, and is accepted by experts of the Department as the largest authenticated brown trout. This remarkable fish was caught on the troll by Colonel J. W. Pepper on 1 September, 1861, in Doorus Bay on Lough Derg; he gave the weight as 30½ lb. The title 'Pepper's Ghost' was attached to this trout by a historical accident, and is not to be taken as suggesting that there is anything apocryphal about it. The original 'Pepper's Ghost' was a stage show that delighted our forbears; it created optical illusions by means of a clever arrangement of mirrors.

The same edition of the *Angler's Guide* (p. 224) declines to include in the list an even larger trout on the ground that "the fish may well have been a salmon". Personally I regret the exclusion and do not find the ground given satisfactory. If one can believe in a 30-lb. trout, one can believe in a 35-lb.

from the lake, and took two and a half hours to play." A trout of 13 lb. weight — imagine what that means in terms of angling. A trout larger than many a salmon, and with better fighting qualities, at the end of your line — imagine what that is to play. For two hours and a half your top-joint is bent like a hoop; any minute he may yield, and give in; any moment the cast or dropper may break under the strain; any moment the hold may give way, and the fly or bait come back to you. They are there, those whoppers, strong as horses, stronger than salmon of their weight, and with more stamina. I have never hooked one *to my knowledge*; but what they were that broke me, I shall never know. I have often seen them out of the water when the lake is low. I have seen one come, head and tail, to my fly, and miss. I have sat in a boat for two hours and a half while my son played one, and I shall now describe the fight. We lost the battle and the fish in the end; for we had no gaff. Had we a gaff in the boat, he was ours; and since then I never venture on Lough Conn without a gaff.

It was Thursday the 22nd day of August, 1943; for the two days previous gales from the nor'west raged, and no boat could put out. On the third day the wind moderated, but was still from the nor'west, with sunshine and light cloud. We set out in the morning from Cloghans in two boats and found the fish unusually responsive. We drifted past Rinevelia, by Friarstown Bay to Sandy Bay. Rounding Rinmore Point we found more north in the wind, and continued our drift southwards. There was a good swell at Brackwanshagh and we landed, made tea and took lunch. The two boats had taken two dozen nice trout between them. After lunch things went slack, as usually happens

trout, and it is hard to believe that sportsmen of those days could not distinguish a brown trout from a salmon. It was taken somewhere near Tuam, it would seem; we are not told where; but it may have come from waters that do not hold salmon. The account is extremely objective. Lady Howth, writing on 6 August, 1736, from Turlaghvan, near Tuam, to Dean Swift, says: "Since I began this there came in a trout; it was so large that we had it weighed; it was a yard and four inches long, twenty-three inches round, his jaw bone eight inches long, and he weighed thirty-five pounds and a half. My Lord and I stood by to see it measured."

after an active morning; but the breeze held and we continued to drift with it to Wilson's Rock and the Cormorants' Rock. Carogora Bay was in the shelter, and some big trout rose. Frank was fishing in the bow, and casting close in shore among the rocks, with a Watson's Fancy on the middle dropper. He saw a great trout come at it deliberately and take. Tom Timlin, the boatman, had seen it too; he seized the oars and pulled frantically towards the deep. The reel screamed, and screamed the louder because it held no great length of line. The first essential was to get him away from the rocks, away from the ground he knew. Once down among those big rocks he would bury himself, or get some purchase on the weeds, or cut the cast or line on some sharp edge.

We reached the deep; the first peril was past. Tom put down the oars, and Frank took stock, and began to recover line. He stood a good chance in the ordinary way; he had a stout rod and a new 1 x cast; let the trout race about in the open; the more he runs the sooner he will tire. But they are very wise, these wise old trout. He made one or two runs, and jumped once or twice near the boat. "My word, what a trout!" Then he settled down to a long sulk. Boring down head first, he took up position at the stern of the boat, immediately beneath it, down deep, and defied all attempts to dislodge him. In that position the strain is reduced to a minimum, and is vertical. Sideways strain, as most anglers know, throws fish off their balance, keeps them uneasy, and tires and finally beats them. When the trout's head is down like a bar of iron, there is no strain sideways, and whatever vertical strain there is is taken by the weight of the body.

There is little more to tell. The two hours and a half passed, but how to convey their passage to the reader I know not; it was just one long, slow drift, packed with hopes and fears; we drifted out into the open lake, with the other boat following to give what help they could; we drifted alongside Glass Island, formerly a centre of poteen making. There we sent the other boat off to see if a gaff could be borrowed; they returned with a curious weapon, a cross between a Bishop's crook and a huge gaff; we heard afterwards that it was used for hauling the bottles from the bed of the lake; but it could not do a gaff's work.

Now we were near the end of the lake. Pontoon with its shallow, sandy bays was well in sight; and we had a difficult decision to make; shall we stay out in the deep and hope to tire him out, or make for the shallows where he will be forced to surface? For over two hours we had played him, and he was still apparently as fresh as ever. So we decided for a sandy bay. The plan would have worked but for one particular that could not be foreseen. We were now in shallower water, and could see the fish plainly. Frank was playing him from amidships. I was at the stern and could almost touch his tail. In the real shallows we could get sideways strain, and then, we hoped, the end would come. The end came in a different way. At the entrance of the bay there was a patch of weeds; in a flash he was in them, got the purchase, and in a minute or so the cast came back to us *minus* the Watson's Fancy. Ten to fifteen pounds was our estimate of his weight. Soon afterwards, so we read in a local paper, the carcase of a large trout was washed ashore in a neighbouring bay. I wonder was it the same fish.

But the last word shall be said by the first actor in the drama. Here are Frank's recollections of the fight twenty years after.

"I still have the most vivid recollection of the dark shape appearing suddenly beside the fly, of my 'strike' that was like straining at an unyielding rock, and of the crescendo of excitement during his first run, culminating in his first jump.

"I often recall the long period of drifting across the deep down to Glass Island, the taut line vibrating through the waves as the boat drifted, the arching rod, and the aching wrists that sometimes made me wonder whether I would be forced to hand the rod to one of the others.

"There were times when the fight became almost monotonous, times when I found my attention wandering from the great trout towards contemplation of the grandeur of Nephin on that day of sunshine and shadow. I can still see the patches of light and shade chasing each other down the steep slopes to the lake, and the vivid, purple glow of the heather above Cornakillew wood.

"And suddenly the reverie would be broken as the great trout hurled himself into the air between us and the sun. We had a fleeting glimpse of the small head, the heavy shoulders, the enormous girth of his body, and the broad tail. A moment elapsed, and once more there was nothing but the taut twanging line, the arching rod, and the rainbow dancing in the spray and splash of his returning dive.

"I can recollect the hopes that dawned when we fancied he began to weaken a little in the shallower water, the horror at the sight of the long weeds trailing beneath us, the final plunge, and the sadness at reeling in the broken cast.

"Last, and perhaps not least, I recall the ten shilling note given by a sympathetic father that went a little way towards healing a broken heart."

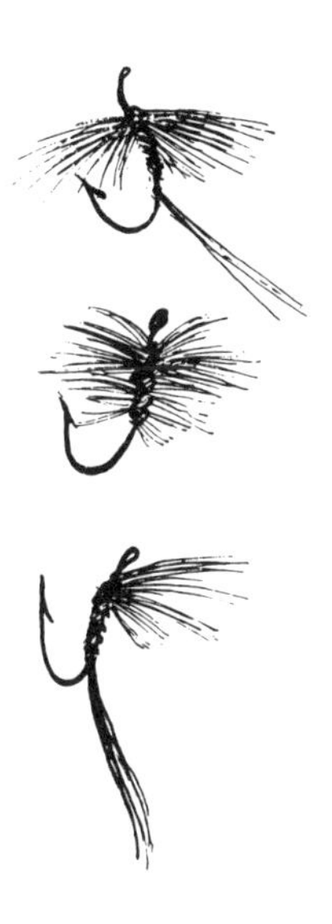

CHAPTER X

DAPPING AND TROLLING

IF, as Solomon thought, "to everything there is a season, and a time to every purpose under the heaven",* then there is a time to dap, and a time to troll, and there is certainly a time to refrain from dapping and from trolling. Dapping and trolling are good servants, but bad masters. If wet-fly fishing is one of the 'minor tactics' of the chalk stream,† then dapping and trolling are 'minor tactics' of the great lakes, at any rate on those lakes where fly fishing holds pride of place.

The very distinction, however, between major tactics and minor tactics is narrow and parochial, and may be called in question from more angles than one. If fishing tactics are *major* and *minor* according as they are more widely employed, or less, what are we to make of the fact that on Lough Sheelin more trout are taken by dapping than in any other way? Probably, too, on the Corrib — that grand expanse of water with an island for every day in the year — more trout are taken on the dap and by the troll than by other methods. Again, if angling tactics are to be classed as major and minor according to some supposed intrinsic superiority and inferiority, we lay ourselves open to the charge of piscatorial

* Ecclesiastes iii, 1.

† G. E. M. Skues, *Minor Tactics of the Chalk-stream*, London, 1910.

snobbery. There is a regrettable tendency to regard our own tactics as major, and the other man's as minor. We may grant, indeed we *must* grant, that on a given lake or river, or at a given time of year, or in some other given set of circumstances, or for a given angler, one type of angling is superior to another type; but superiority of that sort is relative and extrinsic, not absolute or intrinsic. In other words, when contrasting one lawful method of taking trout with another method, all fair-minded anglers will make allowance for time of year and place, for local conditions and rules, and for the age and circumstances of the angler. That done, there can be no manner of doubt that dapping and trolling have their places in the angler's calendar and scheme of things. Those who dap and troll in due measure, at the right time, in the right place, and for a good purpose, have no need to apologize for their methods, or to feel an inferiority complex about them.

Most anglers would prefer to take a trout on wet or dry fly than on dap or troll; there is more active exertion in the former methods, and sometimes, not always, more skill and knowledge. To troll downwind, to dap all day when trout are coming to the artificial fly, to chug, chug, chug all round the lake all day, day in, day out, spring, summer and autumn with trolls out — such practices call for defence, and may in particular cases be indefensible. But Homer sometimes nods, and so does Izaak Walton. Izaak did not always fish to the height of his art. Sometimes he would bait his hook, peg his rod to the river bank, retire to his honeysuckle hedge, and recite poetry to his scholar; then the two of them would go across to the Jolly Mermaid, would drink a bottle of sack and after a sing-song with Maudlin would return to the river, lift the rod and find a fine trout on. That method, to Izaak, was letting the rod fish for you. "Our angles are like money put out to usury,"* he says. Sportsmanship today has outgrown that practice; but we may be permitted to adopt and adapt Izaak's quaint conceit of passive angling, and describe and defend both

* *The Compleat Angler*, I, xii; cf. ibid., I, v, "fishing with a dead-rod".

dapping and trolling as, in large part, letting the rod fish for us.

One of the charms of dapping is its family aspect; it is a family affair, or may be so. With the dapping-rod ladies compete on equal terms with men; many ladies dap better than many men; they have more patience; they let the rod fish for them; if a rise comes, they leave it to the fish, and do not react with a lightning strike. Children, too, can join in, as soon as their little arms can support the rod. Place your young hopeful in the centre of the boat with a dapping-rod, and the two fly rods at bow and stern will be able to work away without inconvenience; and it is on the cards that the youngster will contribute the fish of the day. His mother can take a second dapping-rod, also in the centre, if the boat has five seats (or they can take it in turns). The fly rod needs good casting space, right and left, and there is not room for it in the centre. The set-up of two dapping-rods in the centre, flanked by two fly rods, works well as a rule. If the breeze is fair and steady, the daps go straight ahead, and hardly interfere at all with the casting field. The wealthy uncle must be in the bow where the chances are best; take the stern yourself, and run the engine when it is wanted; the lady and the lad can dap from the centre; and that leaves one seat for the gillie or whoever controls the drift. On a rough day the lady and the lad should be left ashore, and be promised compensation in the form of another day. Dapping is not the most serious or most sporting form of angling; but it gets fish, and large fish; it fits well into the pattern of family life, and is the sauce and the spice of many a pleasant picnic or birthday party.

Some anglers scorn dapping and call it 'the mug's game'; experts dislike it for its passivity, and because fish to be had on the dap can usually (not always)* be had on the wet fly or the dry. But try everything once; without some acquaintance with dapping angling education is incomplete. Collecting bait is troublesome; but it is often good fun, and always

* On a sunny day, when there is a nip in the air, the dap persuades, where the artificial fails.

good exercise; and if your friend has 'snapped' you in the act of grabbing daddies or pouncing on grasshoppers, he has you at his mercy, and will have the laugh of you for a long time to come. The long dapping-rod is a nuisance in a crowded boat. Still and all a little dapping is a great rest for tired arms; it is a pleasant change after a long bout of unrewarded casting; and it is better to get a trout on the dap than not get one at all.

The dap does best in a light breeze, and the rod must be long enough to catch the mere whisper of a breeze; fifteen or sixteen feet is about right; it should be of bamboo or other light material. On a rod of that length a well-hooked fish has no chance; and even three-pounders are swung round without ceremony to the back of the boat. A friend of mine met the situation by mounting a nine-foot rod on a six-foot wooden stock, and dapping from it; when he hooked a fish, he took the rod off the mount, and played him. Dapping tackle consists of twice the rod-length of floss silk, a couple of feet or so of gut or nylon, reasonably strong, and a small eyed-hook. Join one end of the silk to the line and the other end to the gut or nylon with the hook attached. Bait the hook, and the silk floats out in the breeze and lets the dap alight dibble-dibble-dabble on the dancing wavelet. The dap must be closely watched; it may disappear, or a dimple or a swirl beneath it may tell a tale.* The watching is a great strain, which old eyes cannot for long support; and in sunshine dark glasses are essential.

The daps in use at various times of the year and in various places are (1) the mayfly, (2) the daddy-long-legs, *alias* harry-long-legs, (3) the grasshopper, and (4) a mixed grill. If there is a choice, go by the strength of the breeze and the height of the wave. In a very light breeze nothing heavier than a couple of daddies will blow out; you may add one daddy, or even two, if the breeze freshens. A hopper by itself will soon get waterlogged, and will sink; for general use in a good stiff breeze there is nothing to beat the mixed grill, i.e., a hopper garnished by a couple of daddies.

* For conflicting theories of the strike see above (p. 22).

Hopper and daddy are, or should be, little more than adjuncts to fly fishing on the lake in July, August and September. What most anglers and tackle-shops call 'dapping' and think of as 'dapping' is the whole-time, whole-hearted dapping with the mayfly in the mayfly season.

The mayfly (*ephemera danica*), otherwise known as the Green Drake (in its first stage) and as the Black Fly or Spent Gnat (in its second stage), is a large, conspicuous fly of great interest to all who fish and think. The angler actually *sees* its grand mutation that opens long vistas to speculative thought. There is the wriggling shrimp that for two years has lived in the sunless ooze at the bottom of the lake. Hey presto! It is now a winged fly. A moment's pause on the surface, and it wings its purposive and purposed way ashore; for two days it is a denizen of the upper air, an individual. Another change, and back it goes to the water to die and fulfil its being in its kind.

To dappers the mayfly in its season is 'the fly' and has no other name or surname. In many waters its arrival transforms the fishing for a while, and when it goes, the fishing ceases. In some waters, like Lough Sheelin, the fly comes up with a burst; the hatch reaches its height in three or four days, and peters out in three or four weeks. "Fly up fly down" was the historic telegram sent by the man on the spot to the angler in the city. It is useless to go till the fly is up; and once it is up, the news brooks no delay. The hatch sets the big trout wild. On the midland lakes, Sheelin, Derravaragh, Owel and Ennell, the season is short and the hatch intense. On the western lakes the hatch is never so intense, and the season is proportionately longer. On Conn, for instance, one rarely sees the fly in any quantity; one would never think of filling a fly-box; but a small, short hatch-out is to be seen practically every day from the beginning of June to the middle of September.

A book written about one hundred years ago by an English angler visiting Ireland contains the remark,* "There

* I cannot now find the reference.

are now no trout in Lough Sheelin." I smiled when I read the words, and thought of the big rises of trout I have seen there, and of the three five-pounders I took in one half-hour on the dry fly off Church Island. Were the words true when they were written? Were there *then* no trout in Sheelin? Or did the visitor come there when the fly was over? Certainly when I first knew the lake thirty years ago the fishing was over to all intents and purposes when the mayfly hatch was finished. Sheelin then was entirely a mayfly lake. Presumably the bottom-feeding was so rich that nothing short of the luscious drake would tempt the trout to rise. "No trout in Lough Sheelin" — well, it may have been true one hundred years ago; lakes have their cycles; but if the writer of that book could have peered through the mists of the future, he might have seen Goreport Bay alive with trout, when the first big hatch occurs; and if he had been with me at Kilnahard on a certain afternoon when the breeze dropped suddenly, and the black fly first came out in myriads, he would have seen all around the boat for an hour a plunging mass of feeding trout.

The mayfly comes up on many Irish waters; it hatches on the rivers Boyne, Liffey, Slaney and Nore; it hatches on reservoirs;* it is well established on the big lakes, Ree, Derg, Corrib, Mask and Conn; but I doubt if there is a hatch anywhere to equal that on Lough Sheelin. On a grey day there with a light nor'westerly breeze the fly hatched so thick around our drifting boat that we could not find a vacant spot to place our daps. In such a season every hawthorn and ash tree on the shore will be plastered with fly; and on a warm dry evening the air beside the lake and for a mile or two around will be humming with the spinners' Bacchic dance. It is an amazing sight. The ducks and geese from the farms and cottages around the lake come down to the water's edge, and gobble their fill; the farmyard hens and seagulls and dickey birds all take their toll. The trout go

* The late Mr. Bindon Scott and I released a boxful of mayfly from Sheelin on the lower reservoir at Bohernabreena near Dublin. The fly soon established itself there; and in two years there was a noticeable hatch.

mad for a time, and then go down for good, glutted and gorged.

The name *mayfly* is tantalizing, and calls for comment. It is an old name and was well established in Izaak Walton's day; but its derivation and original meaning are not clear. "Oh, it comes up in the month of May," most anglers would say in reply. But does it? Is it a typical fly of the month of May? I cannot speak from knowledge of English and Scottish waters; but in Ireland it is more of a June fly than a May fly. When I knew Sheelin well, the hatch in average years began about 22 May and lasted till the middle of June. When the lilac and laburnum were out in blossom in the suburbs of Dublin, the fly would be up on Sheelin. Lough Derg was a few days earlier, and the other lakes were considerably later;* some hardened dappers would take the lakes in rotation; beginning at Derg, they would go on to Sheelin; thence to Corrib; and thence to Mask.

In view of the fact, then (and I think it is the fact), that in most years and on most Irish waters the bulk of the fly hatches out in June, what explanations can be given of the name *mayfly*? Two explanations have been offered. The first is that the word *may* is not a month, but the hawthorn. The newly hatched fly on a wet and windy day will settle anywhere from a stone to a blade of grass; but in fair weather it is 'choosy', and shows a preference for hawthorn bushes. On this explanation the mayfly is named from the bush *may*, or hawthorn, as the oak fly is named from the oak. There is a similar doubt about the meaning of the word *May* in the wise old saw, 'Ne'er change a clout till May is out'. Is the date-line for the change to be the flowering of the thorn, or the end of the month of May?

The second explanation of the name *mayfly* makes the *may* refer to the month of May in the old, pre-Gregorian calendar,

* These dates are only approximate; and local information should be obtained every year; it is risky to go on chance. The fly is everywhere an uncertain quantity; and the weather of the year affects the date of the hatch. For instance, in the year 1938 spring was early, and was followed by a long dry spell; in that very exceptional year I killed fish on the dap on Sheelin in the last week of April, and the fly was well up there by the first week in May.

which differed from the present calendar by eleven days. In the year 1753 it was provided by Act of Parliament that the day following the first day of September should be known as the twelfth day of September, with consequential changes. Working backwards from that fact one sees that the twelfth day of September in 1752 and earlier years would correspond in real time to what we now know as the twenty-third day of September. Similarly 12 May in 1752 and earlier years would correspond to 23 May, as we now speak. On this reasoning the greater part of the June hatch of fly by present reckoning would have been a May hatch by the older calendar. "Give us back our eleven days," cried the London mob in 1753. If by the same token we give back their eleven days to the Green Drakes of Lough Sheelin, the greater part of the hatch of fly there in an average year would be a hatch of *May*-fly in fact as well as in name; and the 'fly up' telegram would be dispatched annually about 11 May.

And now some thoughts and hints on trolling. The coming of the outboard engine has affected trolling and changed its status. There is now more trolling, and less. There is less casual trolling and more systematic trolling. In former days trolls were almost a necessity to relieve the tedium of the long pull upwind. One pulls a stronger oar when turning an attractive bait, and the music of the reel makes amends for blistered hands. That casual trolling was just an annexe to the drift, and wet-fly fishing on the drift took pride of place in the angler's programme. The long pull upwind and anglers' blistered hands are things of the past, and with them has gone a good deal of casual trolling. Occasionally in a strong head wind one may have to throttle down to avoid splash or straining; and then some gillies let out the troll; but it is hardly worth-while doing so; for trout rarely take in a high wave.

On the other hand what used to be a means to an end has become to some anglers on some waters an end in itself. In its earlier days the engine spluttered and stalled if you slowed down, and refused to start again. Now the outboard has achieved perfection, and permits us to go as we please; we can speed at twenty miles an hour, or chug along quietly at walking pace. We can troll all day with unblistered hands, if we like the game.

Should one like it? I raise the question, and attempt no general answer. Circumstances alter cases. Angling associations are carefully watching the practice, and it needs watching; but so far on the big lakes no serious depletion of stocks, or other ill effects, due to trolling, have been established. The troll catches some trout, and gets rid of some predators. Why should trout-anglers quarrel with either result? If the angler is staying at a bungalow on the lake ten miles from town, and 'living on the country' more or less, he may have to troll a bit to keep the pot a-boiling. Moreover a spot of trolling is a handy way of finding out how the trout are feeling; if there is any move on at all, the troll will get a pluck, if not a pull. Sometimes, indeed, trout will take the fly, when they will not look at the bait, and sometimes *vice versa*; but as a rule if they move to the one, they will move to the other also. There are other good reasons for trolling here and there, now and then; but I confess I am not happy trolling in a fishing breeze; it looks bad, even where it is defensible.

Trolling in a flat calm is a different matter; for it is not in competition with the fly; but is it of any use? Only experience can answer that question; we must troll, and find out. A good deal depends on the time of year and the condition of the fish. In the early spring they are hungry after spawning, and will take the troll freely. In a sudden calm after a storm or during a lull, the troll will work; the trout rush to the surface to see what is up, and are off their guard. The troll will work, too, when you come into a sheltered patch out of the rough. There is a sandy bay on Lough Conn, facing north. Enter it with trolls out against a strong south wind, and as soon as you come under the lee of the land, you are almost certain to get a pull. In a long-continued flat calm on a sunny lifeless day in June, July and August all angling is unproductive, trolling included; it might be worth trying the sharp turn at right-angles, which works wonders at times, and like the googly at cricket, deceives the veteran. The languid trout is following the trolled bait, interested but unconvinced; all of a sudden the bait turns sharply away, and perhaps shows some new beauty of colour or line. "It's alive; it's going to escape me," thinks the trout, and his defences fall.

If all else fails, the troller should try deep trolling in the open; it has been recommended lately; but I cannot speak of it from experience. I tried to try it once, but Michael put his foot down. It is against the tradition of the elders and the customs of the lake. The gillies that connived at it would be chaffed unmercifully at the village Dáil. That august assembly is a gathering of gillies to discuss matters of moment, from international affairs to inter-stellar space, from the price of pigs to today's catch of trout. They meet most evenings when the day's work is done round the hospitable hearth of a confirmed bachelor. The village Hansard might record some such debate as this:

Michael: Well, Tom, I saw you rowing about in the middle of the lake all the afternoon. Were you pitching an eel-line?

Thomas: Bedad, Michael, I was not, and well you know it. I've no use for that trash.

Michael: What were you doing at all, at all? Were you trolling for the sea serpent?

Thomas: Sure, Michael, it's the Major. He says it's the latest thing from London. Deep-water trolling they call it. The Major give me a three-inch Gold Devon and a couple of lead weights. Put them on the line, said he. And I put 'em on. And would you believe it, Michael, he had me pulling up and down the middle of the lake with thon load in tow.

Michael: And did you catch anything?

Thomas: Divil a fin, but a rusty old bucket.

Most gillies dislike trolling deep; to catch in the bottom can be a nuisance, and, worse, a danger; so they go to the opposite extreme; they turn down your best spinning baits, devons and spoons and such like, in favour of light phantoms or wagtails or their own home-made baits of wood, painted and varnished and trimmed with silver paper of varied colour and design. So near the surface do these baits travel that the gulls and terns hover above them and follow them along and sometimes pick them up. We were trolling along Annaghmor, and almost opposite Mossop's Rock (a great lie for salmon) the reel screamed. "It's a salmon," said Michael. The reel kept on screaming. "It's a whale of a salmon," said Michael. The reel screamed as if it would never stop and the green backing began to show. Then I saw him splashing in the shallows, close inshore. "How odd!" said I to myself. "Salmon usually race to the deep, not to the shore." By hard reeling I recovered line; but then the pull began again, and almost stripped the reel, and from a very queer angle. When it stopped, I tightened, and found to my amazement that I was fast in a tree twenty yards in shore. My 'salmon' had taken wings.

In choosing baits for the troll, go by experience and local knowledge. The colour of the water makes a difference, and so does the time of year. The ideal bait is one that takes salmon and trout and pike, but not perch; perch are the trollers' bane. If the water is 'mixed', as the local idiom has it, that is, if there has been a flood down, or a significant fresh, a spoon will take anything that swims. For a warm and sunny day, gold is the favourite colour, and on a dull, cold day blue, or blue and silver.

The *optimum* distance of the bait from the boat is a matter of importance and a matter in dispute. A really hungry fish will take within a foot from the boat, and pike often leave it to the last second. On average a distance of thirty-five yards meets most requirements; at any rate tie a tag of red wool to the line at that distance from the bait, and attach it firmly with size; then you know where you are, and can let out more line, or less, in accordance with conditions. A longer line out increases the danger of sticking in the bottom, and means more time and trouble in reeling in. A shorter line may bring the bait within the splash of the oars or the swirl of the propeller — which, indeed, in some circumstances matters little. A distance of sixty yards has been advocated by English writers for English waters; but that distance is altogether too long for the Irish lakes and would constitute a danger if several boats were trolling in a confined space. Shorten line if passing over shallows, or quicken pace, if it is safe to do so. The two baits should not turn at equal distances from the boat.

Reels for trolling must be capacious, and should have a noisy action, and a strong, adjustable check. Trolling is drowsy work on a warm day, and one needs a reel that talks. Lines must be light, long and strong; in these lakes you never know what you may meet. Professional trollers use long rods; but anglers who troll only as a second string find long rods a nuisance in the boat. A trolling-rod of eight or nine feet in length gives sufficient clearance, and is easily stowed away when out of use. If you are by yourself, be content with one trolling-rod; if he takes, you will have quite enough to do with the one line. If you have another line out, you must get it in before you attend to your fish. Two in a boat can deal effectively with two rods, but no more than two rods. They will be tempted to put out the third bait. Resist the tempter; or the day of reckoning will come. The day will come when you will hit the king of the lake, and while you are frantically wrestling with the third rod, he will race across and make a horrid tangle of all three lines; and you will come home a sadder and a wiser man, *sans* fish, *sans* line, *sans* bait, and perhaps *sans* rod and hope.

The top joint of the trolling-rod should rest against a thole-pin or peg; on the opposite side of the boat from the peg or pin, the butt is fixed securely in the bottom of the boat with its end wedged correctly up against a convenient rib. If the rod is properly fixed, when the fish takes, the rod remains rigidly in place till you are ready to take it up, and only the reel revolves. If it is carelessly placed, the rod will tip over at the strike, and will dance about; the handle of the reel will catch, and a break is as sure as Cocker.

In a very light breeze, too light for drifting, the trolled fly is good, sometimes very good; it takes the small trout. Three flies of lake size and pattern are used; and the trouteens sometimes take greedily. It is not the most sporting of occupations. Char (*Salvelinus colii*) are sometimes taken in this way in Lough Conn. The char is a lovely little fish, good to look at, excellent at table; he is perfectly streamlined, and has the delicate pink hue of a fresh-run salmon.

The western lakes hold large pike; pike come better to the spun bait, but are often taken on the troll; they are moody creatures, and sometimes fearless. The largest one listed in the Irish *Angler's Guide* weighed fifty-three pounds; it was taken on Lough Conn in July 1920 on the troll by Mr. Johnnie Garvin of Cloghans, a friend of mine. In the same lake, spinning from a boat, an English visitor a few years ago took half a ton of pike in three weeks' fishing. The locals who work the nets there for the Inland Fisheries Trust took a sixty-pound pike in 1956 off Carogora bay; they told me they had netted and lost a much larger pike. Pike of ninety pounds weight and upwards are mentioned without much circumstance or conviction in the above-named publication (3rd ed., pp. 212-13). Personally I have no difficulty in believing in the existence and capture of pike of that weight. Two steady young men, well accustomed to the lake and the ways of fish, were working at the hay, not thirty yards from a small bay on Lough Conn. They heard a commotion, and looked over the hedge, and saw a displacement of water far too big for any salmon or trout to make. It was, they told me, as if the whole centre of the bay were heaving up. On Lough Sheelin I myself have seen an enormous pike, at whose weight I could not guess. He looked half as long as the boat. Paddy Briody was with me. We had been dapping there, or trying to dap, on a breathless day in early June. The pitiless sun shone down all day from a cloudless sky; you could boil a trout in the surface water. Towards sunset it cooled off a bit. We were at the Finea end of the lake watching for a rising trout, when this monster surfaced at boat's length from our boat, and cruised slowly around, obviously in difficulties from the heat; Paddy was scared. I was revolted. I raised the oar to hit him on the head, Paddy protesting. The sun was setting behind me; the shadow of the oar fell across the pike; he took fright, and sank, and we saw him no more.

The mere presence of these outsize fish, pike and trout and salmon, and the thought that one of them may be nosing your bait and may seize it at this very moment, add a piquant sauce to the dull game of trolling.

CHAPTER XI

THE SPATE RIVER

"AND I'm using a shpoon, Sir, would pull a trout out of a graveyard, if he were in it." Thus Seán, the local 'poacher', to me across the swollen waters of the river in spate. Pindar's eloquence of old was compared to a turbulent river and Seán's speech, too, when he was moved to it, would borrow from the torrent its rush, and foam and fury. He thought in visual images; he loved quaint similes and eerie metaphors and macabre comparisons; and when he found one that he liked, it seized him, and a spate of words to express it came tumbling from his mouth. Seán was conveying to me with pitying emphasis what I could see for myself, viz., that the fly rod in my hand was useless at present. He with his irresistible spoon could not get a pull; how then could I hope to do anything with the fly?

This was one of the best pools on the little river, and I had hoped for 'first water', and was not best pleased to find Seán there; but I was not surprised; for his house was 'contagious' (as they say) to the river, and as soon as a flood came down in July, August or September, he was on the job, ready with rod, gaff and creel. He loved angling, and was expert at it. Today his victory in the race had done him no good; he had not stirred a fin that morning in spite of his wonderful lure. Glad of a rest he sat down on the driest stone he could find, and we exchanged notes across the flood. It was quite a small river; only some ten yards separated us, and we could hear one another perfectly. "Yes," he said, "it has been a bad season for salmon and trout; and there has been plenty of water for them; it's the nets in the estuary below. What right have them fellows down there to be netting every day of the week, Sunday and all, and with double nets?" I smiled inwardly at his indignant, 'What right . . . ?', and I thought, but of course I did not say, 'And what right have you, Seán, to be fishing here? You have not paid your £2 for a licence.' Then conscience smote me, and I whispered to myself, 'How about you yourself? You have your licence; but is that enough? Have *you* a right to be fishing here?'

Just then, a queer little cut of a man in knickerbockers and worn leather gaiters crossed the gap at the lower end of the field, and bore down upon me. "It's Geordie, the bailiff," said my friend across the water. Geordie advanced, deferential, but determined. "Good day to you, Sir; that's a nice flood down; did you have any luck yet?" "I'm only after starting," I replied, "and my friend there tells me I'm too early with the fly."

"Is it Seán?" said Geordie. "He should know; he's the greatest poacher on the river; aren't you, Seán?"

We all three talked on a while and gossiped about Hitler, and the wet season, and the uncut hay, and the oats laid, and the turf* cut and foot-stacked, but sodden wet. "A lorry-load of it was taken up from here for Dublin the other day, Sir; and it went on fire on the Mullingar road, and was burnt to a cinder — all except the turf." The little joke warmed up proceedings, and Geordie opened his gambit with a remark about 'Dev' and his 'Economic War'. He was trying to find out who I was, and what my politics. I did not rise to the fly, and so without further preliminaries Geordie came to the point, and said, "By the way, Sir, I see you are fishing. Would it be troubling you to let me see your licence? I'm the bailiff."

* *Anglice*, peat.

He took the flimsy piece of paper in his hands, made a show of reading it, folded it up, and handed it back politely, and we resumed our gossip. Did the atom bomb affect the weather? Could the harvest be saved? And so on. Then Geordie looked up at the sun, and said he must go. "I hope you will get a fish,* Sir; but you should try higher up the river. The fish travel fast this warm weather, and you would have a better chance upstream." I knew that opening, too; and to save Geordie further embarrassment, I took the bull by the horns, and asked him, "This is free fishing,† isn't it?" I thought Geordie and Seán exchanged glances and smiles at my innocent question. The former replied, "Free fishing, Sir? Well, it is, and it isn't; in a way it's free; in a way it's preserved. No notices are put up, and visitors often fish here without permission, and so does our friend, Seán, yonder. And I never turn him off, nor anybody else; but the fishing belongs to Major Smyth; it has been in his family for years and years. That's his house up there in the trees. He doesn't fish himself, and he gives leave freely; but he likes to be asked. Why wouldn't you write to him, Sir, if you are staying in these parts? I'm sure it would be all right." I promised to write, and Geordie went off, well pleased with his own tact and tactics, and their happy issue.

I duly wrote to the Major, apologizing for my trespass, and asking permission to fish the river. He replied courteously, giving me leave to fish it as often as I wished, adding, "Please keep anything you catch."

Left to ourselves Seán and I resumed our conversation; for the river was still brown. He attacked me over my promise to Geordie. "You've no call to do that, Sir. The Major's a decent man, and I wouldn't say a word against

* On a spate river a 'fish' always means a salmon or grilse, and a 'trout' always means a sea-trout, otherwise called a 'white trout'. The resident trout are rarely mentioned; they are just 'brownies', and are mostly mere pinkeens. If you catch any worth frying, the cottager's children where you park your car will be glad of them.

† The cautious definition of 'free fishing' given in the *Angler's Guide to the Irish Free State* (Dublin, 1937, 3rd ed.) is "waters over which the legal owners of the fishing rights, whether riparian proprietors of land or others, do not at the time of writing evince any disposition to exercise their rights to the exclusion of anglers".

him personally; but the fishing is no more *his* than it's yours or mine; it's free for all." I held my whist. Seán may have been disputing fishing rights in general; but more probably it was a local dispute about title, perhaps going back a long way and mixed up with other things. Clearly the Major was in possession, and had nine-tenths (*plus*) of the law on his side. I looked at Seán's tall, lithe figure, and noted his ease of movement. There were bearing and poise beneath his rough exterior and homely speech; perhaps his forbears had lived in that house among the trees once upon a time.

The conversation ended abruptly; for suddenly we both spotted what we had long been looking for — foam suds. When the white and yellow clumps of foam suds, puffed and swollen like yeast, break off from the banks in the little bays and backwaters, and float away downstream, anglers must be up and doing; it is a sure sign that the river is falling, and the brown water beginning to clear. Seán went back to his house for his fly rod, leaving me in possession of the pool, and before he returned I had grassed a grilse with forked tail, up that morning with the sea lice on him, fresh as a daisy, gleaming with the iris of the salt sea waves.

That evening in my easy chair in front of the fire I tried to think out the problem of 'poaching' with reference to the special conditions of the spate river. There are three separate questions: the licence to fish in the district, the right to fish the river, and access to the river bank. The last two questions are in practice tied up together from the nature of the case. Offences in respect of the licence, or of the fishing rights, or of the use of the river bank are commonly referred to as 'poaching' indifferently, but they should be kept distinct. In my eyes Seán was the poacher; for he had no licence. In his eyes I was the poacher; for I did not belong to the district, and did nothing for it, and used his fields and gates and gaps. Major Smyth from the bow window of his drawing-room commands a view of his stretch of the river, and if he had seen us chatting, he would have said, or thought, "There's old Seán at it again! And who's that other angler on the opposite bank?" In his eyes we both were poachers;

for we were after *his* fish; and Geordie who works for him thinks with him. Yet no harsh words had passed; harsh judgments or actions seemed out of place; for each party had a good deal to say for his point of view, and where fishing on spate rivers is concerned, it is often hard to get a clear picture of the moral issue, and not infrequently the legal position, too, is in doubt.

About the licence there is not room for two opinions. To fish for game fish, salmon and sea trout, without it is poaching. All who 'love virtue and angling' will take out the licence and carry it with them. The watching of the spawning-beds, the reporting of flax-water pollution, poisoning and other malpractices, the inspection of licences, and all the other necessary work of the Conservators, cost money, and fishery rates and the fees from rod and net licences are often the only monies at the disposal of the Boards. I tackled Seán about it one day later in the season when I knew him better. He had just landed a fine fish — which made things easier. He was apologetic. He used to take out the licence, he told me, and he intended to do so next year; but he had been hard hit by 'the Economic War', and found it hard to raise the wind. There is often more to it, however, than inability to pay. Seán and his like get so little, comparatively, for their two pounds, and they have a sense of grievance if they pay it. The spate river is up today and down tomorrow; often a whole month will pass without any fishing being possible. In an average season (July to September) Seán might expect ten or twelve fishing days in all; while on a big river or lake a salmon angler might expect to find fishing almost every day from March to September. The one pays two pounds, licence fee, for twelve days' angling; the other pays the same amount for, say, two hundred days' angling. Licences at a reduced fee, covering a short continuous period, are available for visitors, and one could wish that a similar reduction were available for residents, like Seán, who fish a spate river occasionally and discontinuously; but there are administrative difficulties, chief of which would be that of defining a spate river. From the payee's end it does seem unfair that the charge for twelve fishing days should be the same as for two hundred; the unfairness is probably unavoidable, but it is one of the reasons why the local angler jibs at the licence fee and earns the title 'poacher'.

The occasional character of the fishing in spate rivers makes difficulties for the owners of the fishing rights. The limited amount of angling available and its unpredictability detract enormously from the commercial value of the fishing. The big river has strong, constant head-waters and a long, winding course to the sea; it will be fishable almost every day in the season irrespective of the weather. In the Moy, for instance, record catches of salmon, as many as twenty or thirty fish per rod per day, have occurred in low water in June or July. The Moy has a steady flow, rain or no rain; it admits migrants at every tide; it takes two or three days often to rise after rain, and three or four days to fall. Such rivers — and with them are to be counted some major spate rivers with long holding pools — are commercial propositions; they furnish regularly fish for the markets and fishing for anglers; on such fisheries many livelihoods depend. The angler who fishes such waters without leave or payment is truly a poacher, whether he hails from the near-by cottage or is a gentleman from the city who stops his car at the bridge, cannot resist the invitation of the smiling ripples of the stream, and puts up his rod.

The spate rivers proper in respect of their inland waters, are not commercial propositions. No livelihoods depend on them. The nettings in the short estuary may help one or two families to live; but the fish that pass the nets and are taken in the inland waters are taken for the most part by occasional anglers who fish for sport and have little interest in the commercial value of their catch. Owners of fishing rights in a spate river who fish themselves are naturally concerned to keep their rights alive and recognized; but few of them would think it worth-while, even if they could afford it, to incur the expense of a whole-time watcher, and of the rest of the machinery of thorough preservation and enforcement. Owners who do not fish themselves have little motive for bothering about fishing rights, and their rights tend to slumber and sleep. Where spate rivers are concerned, neither owners of rights nor anglers for fish can plan far ahead. The former cannot let the fishing for, say, the coming August, because the latter dare not take the fishing for August (or he will not do so *twice*); the river bed may be bone dry the whole month. To put it bluntly, there is no money in the fishing rights of a small spate river; and naturally those rights become first dormant and then doubtful. With the lapse of time enforcement becomes virtually impossible. In addition to the local odium that in general attaches to enforcement, there is often a real doubt, that can only be cleared up at considerable expense, as to the ownership, particularly when the property changes hands often. And behind the legal question lurks the moral question, and the thinker cannot escape the duty of examining the basis of the particular laws. God placed the fish in the rivers and sends them to the sea and back, and there is precious little that Major Smyth, with the best will in the world, can do about it. Fishery rights are in general defensible, and honest anglers respect them; but spate rivers are to some extent a special case. The owner of fishing rights in them can do practically nothing to maintain and improve the stock of fish, and he often admits the fact by neglecting the fishing. It is not surprising then that local opinion often holds that fishing rights in spate rivers are abstract and artificial, and not on a par with concrete rights to the fruits of labour.

Such is the background to the question of 'free fishing' as the writer meets it in the west of Ireland. In strict legal theory all fishing is, I am told, owned by someone; but there is plenty of fishing in respect of which the owners do not bother to exclude anglers, or in respect of which there is a doubt as to the ownership, as in the case of the large lakes. Such fishing is for practical purposes 'free fishing'. A historical complication is the fact that when the big landlords of the west sold their lands under the Land Acts, in some cases they reserved the sporting rights, in some cases not. Under the later Land Acts the Land Commission, too, varied its practice; sometimes they kept the fishing rights; sometimes they vested them in the tenants along with the riparian lands. The result is that one cannot know for certain without making full inquiry from the Land Commission whether the fishing is owned by the old landlord or by the Irish Land Commission, or by the tenant.

What then is the visiting angler, duly licensed, on holiday in the west country to do who finds himself in a country town near a spate river on a pouring wet afternoon in July or August? Fishing that day is out of the question. Let him spend the rest of the day in making inquiries that will stand him in good stead tomorrow. Is the fishing in the spate river free? Responsible people in the locality will tell him. The local clergy or the guards should know; the hotel and the tackle shop, if there is one, will almost certainly know; the post office may know. If two or more of these sources say, '*Nihil obstat*', let the angler take it as the green light, and go ahead with his plans, including a reconnoitring visit to the river. The situation may change slightly from season to season. An owner may wish to preserve his fishing one year, and not another. But if the angler has made all reasonable inquiries and received what appears to be satisfactory information, for the rest let him 'fish and find out'. If he is turned off, let him go with a good grace and with the measure of apology due. Consideration is usually given to the considerate. If it happens that the angler is asked not to come again, he will in all probability be asked courteously, and will be told to finish his day and keep his catch. Notice boards are usually reliable, but they are not frequent on such rivers.

Here we may leave these troublesome questions about fishing rights and laws and keepers and bailiffs, and give ourselves up to the pure joy of a day on a spate river. For its variety and sense of adventure, and, often, for its spice of excitement, there is no angling in these islands quite like it.

A day on a spate river after a night's rain is normally divided into three parts, viz., (1) no fishing, (2) spinning with bait, and (3) fly fishing. Success depends very largely on the angler's ability to judge the state of the water and on knowing when to pass from bait to fly.

You reach the river, we will say, about 10 a.m. and find that yesterday's trickle of water is now a brown, foaming torrent, over its banks, thick as pea soup, whirling down leaves and grasses, sticks and branches, and all the flotsam of a long, dry summer. Peg a stick in a sandy slope to mark the height of the water; go back to your car and read or write, or, if you play chess, take your pocket set and play over Anderssen's 'Immortal' or one of Capablanca's masterpieces. Come back to the river in an hour or so. Be too early rather than too late. A spate river falls rapidly in a dry season, though not as rapidly as it can rise in a dry season. If a wide catchment area up the mountains is hard-baked, and a torrential downpour occurs, saturation point over that area is reached all in a minute, and down comes the flood literally *all in a minute*. Children should not be left at play unattended beside the most innocent-looking mountain stream. There is a rivulet that enters Lough Mask in Tourmakeady. I was trouting there one day; the water was dead low and gin clear. I climbed the high bank to change a fly; the change made, I looked down, and, lo, the tiny rivulet had turned into a raging torrent.

To fish in a *rising* flood is almost useless, except perhaps in its very early stages, when the fresh water stirs into activity fish that came up in a previous flood; if they think of running without beginning to run, they may take you. When running they do not take, unless *per accidens*; the spawning impulse is strong; they have a long way to go; falls to climb; hazards to overcome; and their time is short.

The falling flood is the angler's chance; for then the fish may rest, and take. When the mark shows that the river is falling, or is on the turn, have the spinning-rod ready. The colour of the water, as well as its height, must be studied in choosing baits. Bog water is clearer than it looks, and fish can see far in it. While the water is brown to muddy, the fly is almost useless; but a big Silver Doctor or Dusty Miller, swinging round into the slack, might stand a chance. When the worst of the 'dirt' has passed, and the water is losing its muddy look, that is the time to make a start with spinning-rod and bait. If grasses are still coming down, you must wait; they twine round the trebles; a few leaves do no harm. The spoon is the best all-round bait for heavy water. Begin with a large spoon, copper and silver, well polished with a good flash; some like the trebles at the head of the spoon, some at the tail; weight the trace at your discretion and at your peril. Try lighter spoons and other baits — devons, collies, phantoms and plug baits — as the flood goes down. Bait fishing on a spate river is something of an art. Accurate and intelligent casting is required, and a considerable amount of knowledge and imagination. You are spinning for travelling fish on their way upstream and pausing to rest. Imagine yourself in their position, and have an eye for likely spots. Search the far bank, overhung though it be with briars and brambles; let the bait take a full swing round, and draw it slowly up close in to the near bank; the big sea trout lie there, and they may snap just as you are lifting. That rowan tree, gay with scarlet berries in autumn, leans over the water like the tower of Pisa; it makes a likely lie, but the cast is dangerous; for a salmon you must chance that moil of waters in midstream behind the big rock. Bring replacements; almost certainly you will need them. Cast with caution and courage; but if you cast courageously, you are bound to lose baits. Even when you know the water well, you will occasionally be snagged; so fish as deep as you dare, and do not count the cost. He who fears to catch in the bottom deserves to catch no fish. "I'm shtuck in the Republic," cried Mick one day. Do not grudge the hospitable 'Republic' a spoon or two. Experience teaches. That inch of twig above the water under the far bank looks innocent enough. Avoid it. Experience will teach you when to reel fast, when slow, when to let the bait down, and when to keep it up; but angling experience, like other goods, costs money and must be bought and paid for.

If you do snag, do not lose your head, and you may not lose your bait. Keep taut, but not tight. To pull hard or to jerk is to drive the hook home in most cases; your aim is to loosen it, and eventually to tease it out. So *suaviter in modo* is the order of the day. First try 'angling' the pull, i.e., pull from different angles. Keeping the line taut, so that it cannot loop round a rock, walk slowly *downstream*, straining gently all the time, feeling (as it were) for the angle of entry and exit. If you are lucky and find the right angle, out comes the bait sweetly; then reel hard lest you snag again.

If that method fails, try the 'traveller'; he works wonders sometimes, and is an artist at his work. He travels for you where you cannot go, and applies your pull where it is most needed, namely at the sticking-point. The 'traveller' can be anything that floats well, and is not too light and not too heavy. An empty bottle, corked, is good; a solid, well-dried stick about four feet long is better. A piece of string about a yard long is tied to the stick so as to divide it unequally, like Plato's line. The other end of the string is tied to some small object that can run freely down the line. A Ω releaser is best for the purpose; a piece of wire bent to shape will do, or a pliant osier, bent round the line and tied. It is an aesthetic joy to watch the 'traveller' setting out on his errand of mercy; you start him upstream of the snag, and he moves downstream and out from the bank with slow dignity at first, gathering momentum as he reaches mid-stream, and then with a sudden plunge he dashes into the whirlpool milling round the snag; there he swings left and right, up and down, seeking the point of exit for the hook, and often finding it. The reason for dividing the stick unequally is now clear; it ensures the maximum range of swing.

If the 'traveller' fails, there is nothing for it but brute force, intelligently applied; pull for it, but pull wisely; put the rod down to spare the top joint; get as near the snag as you can, to save as much tackle as the fates allow; pull steadily without jerking; hope for the best, and if you get everything back, put something extra in the plate next Sunday, and examine your hook in case it has straightened out.

If he takes you, anything may happen, and you must be

ready for anything. Caesar in action had to do everything all at once; the spate river angler 'in a fish' is like Caesar in that respect. On some established fisheries the angler blows his whistle, and a helpful gillie comes; here you are alone with destiny and your hopes and fears; you must work out your own salvation, and the dice are loaded in favour of the fish.

No two fish behave alike; no two pools are alike. Some fish are tired from their run, and meekly bore and cruise and play no tricks; and then it is only a question of time and patience and a landing-place. Others are all fireworks; they are fighting mad from the word 'Go'. The first few seconds are commonly the worst; in that high water fish take terrifically; be sure that trace and line can take the 'take'; the reel must run free, but not free enough to overrun and 'bird's-nest'; if the handle catches on the sleeve of your coat, you are done. Recover slack line, and get him 'on the reel'; then he may let you pause and take stock. What is he? A salmon or a trout? Of what size? Gaff or net? Where are the danger-points and where can I land him? The banks are mostly as nature made them; they are fenced with bushes and briars and ash saplings, hedged with tall ferns and matted bracken and ivy pendants trailing to the river brim. The more obstacles for the angler, the more protection for live-stock, and the better pleased are their owners. Still and all, nature, aided by generations of anglers, usually contrives one gap per pool; if there is literally no gap or other landing-place, we should have given that pool a miss, and deserve what is coming to us.

A hooked sea trout of two pounds weight, or under, is likely to jump three times *simultaneously* (as it seems) in different parts of the pool, and then submit. With salmon and grilse and the large sea trout there is no knowing. Keep your fish moving if you wish him to be yours. A steady strain and a well-timed pull will let him know who's master. Leave no slack line. Your wrists are aching for a rest and your arms do not belong to you; but hold on; he'll give in. Never let him sulk at the bottom; if he does get down among the rocks, and you cannot move him, or even feel him, there is only one remedy; it is an off-chance; it is a heroic remedy, calling for the courage of Hector and the patience of Job; but it works sometimes. Leave down the rod; relax the strain; light a cigarette; you never wanted that particular fish; then hope and pray the spell will work; he will come out sometimes *proprio motu*; if he does come out, it is a wonderful thrill, like the sun at midnight; there's a twitch in the line; see, it moves; it rises; it floats to the surface of its own accord; try not to let it go down again. If the cigarette is finished, and he has not come out, abandon hope of him; pull, and have done with it, and start afresh.

Jonathan Swift, Dean of St. Patrick's, author of the *Drapier Letters*, *Gulliver's Travels*, and much else, went to school at Kilkenny College, then 'the Eton of Ireland', under the shadow of the great castle of the Ormondes at the bend of the River Nore. He was fishing there one day, he tells us, and he hooked "a great fish"; but just as he was landing it, "it slipped back in". Later in life reflecting on the incident the great Dean saw it as a parable and an unhappy omen; for he fished much then in the troubled waters of English politics; he fished for a bishopric, and a bishopric he hooked, a great one; but just as he was landing it, "it slipped back in".

Many a salmon is lost 'at the gaff'; many a fine trout, almost netted, 'slips back in'; many a failure was almost a great success. To enlarge on Swift's parable is tempting; but for the angler on the job it is no parable; it is a stubborn and unwelcome fact. He is alone on a lonely river at the crisis of an angler's day. 'His fish' is almost his, but not quite. There are slips ''twixt cup and lip', and angling battles are lost when all but won. The long strain weakens the hold of the hook; or the sight of net or gaff nerves the fish to make a last despairing bid for life and liberty. Be patient; if his head is down, he is not ready. Be patient, no matter how long it takes. The tyro jabs and grabs at him down below with net or gaff; it is a sure way to lose him; he will come up and surrender when he has to; till then be patient, and bide your time. He may lie on the surface thrashing, and may look at your mercy, and then a practised gillie with a capacious, long-handled net might net him thrash and all; but if you are by yourself, better wait a little longer. When the moment of victory arrives, you will know it; till then be calm and cool, collected and — *resigned.* If netting a largish fish with a smallish net, go for his middle term with the *centre* of the net; his 'extremes' (as logicians say) should slip in at the lift. If gaffing on a high and sloping bank, distrust a narrow ledge at the edge; to have him out there is not enough; he could easily, like Swift's fish, 'slip back in'; carry him to the top of the bank before you relax: and, of course, no sportsman denies his gallant foe the *coup de grâce*, or delays it.

Spinning on the spate river has its attractions and thrills; it yields results when no other method will do so; but in itself it is rather a mechanic art; the angler can put little of himself into it; the fish does all — or nothing. Skill and knowledge and adaptability are required for playing a fish on a spinning-rod, but the hooking of him is largely a matter of luck, or at least owes little to the angler. For conscious artistry, intrinsic charm and delicacy of execution, spinning is not to be compared with fly fishing. The fly rod is a responsive, expressive instrument, like a violin; the artist-angler puts into it his thoughts and desires and something of his feelings. Beside a good fly rod the best of spinning rods is a club or shillelagh.

The cream of the day, its purest joy, begins, usually after lunch, when the white and yellow suds of foam begin to go downstream. Your morning level-mark is now high and dry, and the brown water has become wine, like Homer's 'wine-dark' sea. It is foolish to make a change as long as the bait is working; but if you have had no pull for half an hour, it is time to take stock. In judging the colour of the water allow, as mentioned above, for the natural hue of the turf (or peat, as it is called in England). That colour is always there. The qualities of Jordan were not in Abana and Pharpar, rivers of Damascus; nor is the clear water of the Test and the Itchen in the spate rivers of Connemara.

It is now 'fly water'. Spinning-rods and baits may be left in the car; they will not be wanted again today.* The fly rod for a spate river should be a sturdy trout rod, ten feet long; it has to deal with summer salmon which are mostly small, and with sea trout, large and small. The cast too must meet this dual purpose; it should have three flies, and neither more nor less than three. The salmon fly may be on the bob or the tail; the other two places should go to sea trout flies; but fish are no respecters of box-labels; salmon take trout flies freely, and the littlest trout will take the largest salmon fly. For patterns and size go by the height of the water and local information. Pattern matters little in high water. As the water drops, you shall go down in size, and have more regard to pattern. The following note from my diary names a typical team of flies, which proved very satisfactory because all three contributed to the morning's catch:

> *26 July, 1957:* Fished the river. Nice fresh down, no flood; good fly water; morning bright and breezy; nor'west; six sea trout, total seven pounds, before lunch; met no salmon unless the big sea trout I hooked and lost was a salmon;† Connemara Black (bob), Blue and Silver (middle), Silver Doctor (tail). Fished with one hand, and picked wild raspberries with the other; pleasant morning.

The afternoon of that day turned bleak, but before the fish went completely off the rise, two more sea trout and a grilse were added to the bag. The total is nothing to what some rivers could furnish and some anglers would expect; but it is typical of an average 'good day' on an Irish spate river. Its disappointing feature was the small size of the sea trout. In a good July flood we expect a trout or two of three or four pounds weight. But this was a 'fresh' and not a flood; and no doubt there was not enough water down to tempt the big trout to run.

* Take this rule with a grain of salt. In thundery weather the river can rise and fall twice and thrice a day.

† This convenient phrase is philosophically correct; for what is *subjectively* a trout may be *objectively* a salmon; i.e., the angler may play it as a trout, and find it is a salmon.

Salmon and sea trout up from the sea are as sensitive to weather conditions as are the brown trout of the lakes. Brine and the absence of it have made little difference to ancestral habits. The bright and breezy morning, mentioned above, was followed by an afternoon of gathering clouds and threatening rain, and the pools, responsive in the morning, went dead. When the breeze veers from nor'west to nor'east sea trout, like brown trout, go off the rise; if the change is the other way about, both species tend to come on the rise. If the breeze falls altogether, and a few drops of warm rain patter down, salmon and sea trout* come up to see what is happening, as their fresh-water cousins do, and that is the time to expect a pull. The migrants dislike strong, gusty winds, as brown trout do. Migrating fish, from the nature of the case, are peculiarly sensitive to the strength of the current; and the angler needs to keep the fact in mind. Resting sea trout like long sheltered flats where the current is neither too fast nor too slow; and the angler's job is to find the sheltery spot with the *optimum* flow. Fresh-run fish take better at the tail of the pool. Fish that are up some time lie back in daytime, and come up to the head of the pool in the evening. In the sharps only the smaller sea trout, known as harling, are to be found, as a rule.

'Work' the fly for sea trout; the 'working' brings out all its latent charms, and shows off its colours and the delicate tracery of its feathers; each twinkling fibre vibrates, and the whole fly comes alive. Draw it *across* stream as much as possible, angling the cast according to the current, allowing for its ever varying flow. The whole team of flies should move in a broad sweep, and should swing well round to your side before the reel-in. A trout may be following it, interested and half-convinced, or he may be lying under the bank at your feet, and he often takes at the last moment before the lift. If salmon are in evidence, a loop of line should hang free from the reel, the length of the salmon's girth; if

* Off the coast of Newfoundland the ocean suddenly went flat calm, and a few drops of rain fell; immediately a great whale rose and spouted a hundred yards or so from our ship.

he feels the hook and the check before he has turned and gone down, he has a better chance of getting off. Brown trout anglers when fishing for salmon and sea trout tend to strike too quickly and too hard. On a spate river it is scarcely necessary to strike at all; a twitch to tighten is enough.

Given good fly water after a good summer spate, and given the fish in the mood, the active angler should have a memorable afternoon and evening. An active angler is one who does not 'stay put', but goes with fly rod from pool to pool perhaps two or three miles up- or downstream. Its variety is the special charm of this type of angling, the theme that makes it memorable. The flow of the water is very varied, with consequent variety of casting. The pools are of very varied character; some are long, some short, some circular; they are broad or narrow, open or hedged and overhung; they are deep or shallow, sharps or flats or mixed; in consequence there is great variety in playing, landing and losing fish. And there is great variety of incident; here the wave lifted the salmon, played-out, on to a ledge of rock, and I took him without net or gaff; in that pool I took two three-pounders at one cast, and landed both; in yonder tiny bath of a pool my companion entered the water with a pair of scissors and snipped off bob-fly and middle dropper, before we dared to let down the played-out salmon into the tiny trout net. The incident in angling is usually a private and personal, but a treasured, possession. It may be of no general interest; it may not be instructive; it may not bear re-telling even within the family circle; but you never forget it; it marks with a white stone the day or the place; it is the pearl in the mysterious oyster of memory; round it gather and crystallize the memorable things in an angler's day. These memorable things are visual and auditory images, mental photographs of the pool or scene, echoes of the soughing wind and roaring torrents, or of the whispered babbling of still waters. In memories of the spate river olfactory images have their special place; for the tart tang of bogland and the scents of the aromatic shrubs are pungent in memory; they are more like actual sensations than memory images; they make the mind re-live the happy incident, and not merely remember it.

Casting the fly on the clearing water of a spate river is delicate work, calling for accurate aim and sure touch; if the wind is high or gusty (and it is usually high and gusty the day after heavy rain), casting will tax the powers of an expert. The far bank, often hedged and overhung, must be searched; for close in under that bank he lies; cast two inches too far, and you catch the bushes; cast short, and you miss your mark. Do you see those two rocks in midstream; between them, like Scylla and Charybdis, you must deftly guide your team of flies, risking a snag to hook the fish of your dreams, the 'not-impossible' him or her. Beneath yonder swift, smooth slide of water King Salmon lies with tail gently swaying to the current, unsuspecting, "the world forgetting, by the world forgot"; send your fly teasingly over the spot, and he may be yours. Greased line methods have small scope in these small streams; still fish your best; fish as if you were fishing the lordly Moy under the critical eye of the master gillie. 'Mend your line' all you can. Present the fly before the line, as far as currents and cross-currents permit. Sympathy with your instrument is perhaps the rule of rules. Feel your slender, nervous rod as an extension of your arm, and feel your silk line and nylon cast and dainty fly as extensions of your rod; then by power of will and intention place the luscious morsel on the surface of the stream at the desired spot, ten, fifteen, twenty yards away; there let it fall like thistledown, as falls the fancy on the perfect phrase. When you have done that, you have graduated *Magister in Artibus* (*Piscatoriis*), and have achieved the philosopher's dream, action at a distance, or have come as near doing so as is given to mortal man.

King Salmon is the star-turn of the spate river. The sea trout (*salmo trutta*) are his courtiers. There are more sea trout in the average run of most rivers, and on the whole they take more freely. Some of them are as large as small salmon, and more lively. The two species are distinct; a salmon is not a sea trout, but to say which is which will tax the knowledge of even the experienced angler; they look alike in the river, on the bank, and at table. External colour is no guide, especially if the fish has been up some time in fresh water. The sea trout's flesh is lighter pink; the posterior edge of his jaw is situated behind the level of the eye, whereas in *young* salmon it is situated directly below the eye. The scales, however, furnish the only really satisfactory mark of distinction. The salmon has eleven rows of scales in oblique line from the adipose dorsal fin to the lateral line; whereas the sea trout has fourteen rows of scales.

Sea trout are queer, unpredictable, crotchety things, more so than salmon, more so than brown trout. Even when fresh-run they sulk; they sulk even when the overhead conditions are good. They sulk hour after hour for no apparent reason, and they 'come on', too, for no apparent reason. You say to yourself, "There's not a fish in the river. I'll have ten more casts, and then give it up." Perhaps the tenth cast will give you a fish, and then they may 'come on with a bang'. For the longer the sulk, the nearer the rise. On a normal July day when the water is clearing quickly after a good flood, one may look for a rise about 4 p.m. If it does not happen then, wait on till 6.30 p.m. or later. Unless the evening turns cold or thundery, the great moment will come. It may come when the white moth appears; the dead river suddenly springs into life. Trout, taking trout, are everywhere; the long deep flats are full of them, large ones; half-pounders are in the shallow runs; pounders, two-pounders, three-pounders and upwards are at the head and the tail of every pool, and in the middle, too. Your bag, empty all day fills in an hour; it is heavy on your back, but it lightens your heart, and you trudge back to your car, tired out, but triumphant.

And now a word about the third and fourth dimensions of the spate river. We see it as a surface in length and breadth; but its depth is important, too; depth is perhaps more important in the spate river than in other angling waters; for, as mentioned above (p. 159), the landing-place is often the great difficulty in these wild parts; with all the undergrowth uncleared and unchecked, and overhanging trees uncut, it is hard to bring a hooked fish to book from the bank, and the angler is tempted to go in after him with net or gaff. Dare he do so? Plato, who knew more than most about the dimensions of the world in which we live, thought* that there is only one way to get to know a river, and that is to enter it and walk up and down in it. The bed of a spate river is an uncertain quantity; here it is easy walking on firm and gravelly bottom; here you must stumble and scramble over slippery rocks with deep holes between them; there again the bottom is neither gravel nor firm sand nor stone nor rock, but treacherous, unsubstantial mire, yellow mud or black bog. The angler, if he can, should take Plato's advice; go when the water is low; walk up and down in your favourite pool, and you will learn where you can tread in safety and where danger lies. But no matter how well you know the river, never enter it in brown flood; the higher your waders, the greater the risk; no fish is worth the risk. As long as the water is fit for spinning it is not safe to enter. When the turn of the fly rod comes, the water is lower; its turbulence has passed; it is beginning to clear; and if you can see the bottom, and know it to be firm and gravelly, it is safe to enter; even so, care must be exercised; rocky pools are not safe, nor are deep, soft, boggy flats.

You are fighting a strong fish, as well as a strong current; when you are standing in the water it is often hard to see what to do, and harder still to do it. The current is tugging at your feet. The light is going, and you can only guess the whereabouts of your fish by the bend of the top joint against the sky; and if it is daytime, and a dazzling July sun is beating down, every wavelet becomes a blinding stab of light. Even when your fish is played out and the light reasonably good, netting is by no means easy. You are not on *terra firma*; unconsciously you are feeling for a foothold, and both hands are under strain. He is lying beat on top of the water; now's the time; with the right hand draw him over the net; alas, at the critical moment the left hand

* *Theaetetus*, 201.

falters; the current pulls the net just out of position; the rim hits the fish; he slithers out on the wrong side; the shock gives him a second wind; his struggles start all over again. Now he is quiet once more; no mistake this time; in he comes towards the gape of the net, and as the net dips to receive him, your left hand is as steady as the northern star; but as you lift with your left, you relax with your right; again the fish is a few inches downstream; again the rim hits him; again you miss your kill.

This part of the day's work is, of course, child's play, if you have a gillie in attendance; he will net the fish neatly, carry the bag and the lunch and make things easy for you. But is a gillie in place here? The fishing is on so small a scale; the surroundings are so wild and unconventional. An established fishery has its dignity and sense of ordered ease. Each pool is named; each beat has its recognized limits, measured to a foot. There are stands and built-out platforms and huts where you may take your luncheon and seek refuge from the rain. There the capable gillie, drilled in the routine of the day, is in place, and he often adds greatly to the pleasure and profit of the day. But the spate river is different; on it the gillie, for one angler at least, is a luxury somewhat out of place. The spate river is a solitary place, and solitude is part of the spirit and charm of angling there. Let me be alone in these lonely places, alone with my joys and sorrows, alone with victory and defeat, alone with my long, long thoughts. Here are no huts, no stands, no stiles, no comforts, and hardly any works of man. It is heavy going; we must watch each step; splashing through bogs, stumbling over tussocks, we shall be tired out by the end of the day; but the air is champagne and carries us through. We are "up the airy mountain and down the rushy glen". The fairies are near. We are in the wide open spaces of the four-dimensional world of sense and spirit.

Overhead the lone, black raven utters his 'serious call', and the cheerful curlew whistles a reply; in the dykes and ditches stand the royal ferns, six feet high, the stately osmunda; the hedges flame with fuchsia, hung with crimson drops; the dark-green hazel bushes are laden with nuts; all around are white moon-daisies and blue cornflowers, clover and rag-wort, the gay montbretia, fluffy white bog-cotton, dainty heartsease, the graceful grass of Parnassus, and the purple honeyed heathers, some with big bells, some with small. The poor, black, barren bogland is amazingly rich in aromatic scents; the fragrance of myrtle and sweet-gale fills the air; here are mint and thyme, ling and meadow-sweet, and many herbs that are good to smell.

In all this beauty of colour and form, of sight and sound and smell, deep calls to deep through sense; and those anglers who have time to spare for the spirit of their pastime and the *genius loci* and the poetry of spate-river angling will enhance their enjoyment of the day, and will enrich their memories with pleasures that may last for life. In these surroundings we are in a four-dimensional world; body and spirit are free; we can go where we like and think what we like. We fish a long line, and think long, long thoughts. Human life and its setting lie open to contemplation. The salmon and trout, fresh up that day from the sea, bring with them the glamour, romance and mystery of the deep. "Thy way is in the sea, and thy path in the great waters, and thy footsteps are not known."* So the sacred poet sang to God three thousand years ago. And these creatures of God that move in the great waters, move, like Him, in a mysterious way. Their footsteps too in the sea are still not known; and perhaps that is part of the reason why a day on a spate river, more than most angling days, lifts the veil of nature and shows the thoughtful angler something of its meaning and value and Source.

* Psalm lxxvii, 19.

CHAPTER XII

THE ETHICS OF ANGLING

THE ethics of angling is sometimes called in question. Angling is said to be a cruel sport. That is the central charge, affecting us all. Anglers are charged also with wasting time, with neglecting serious things, with fishing to excess, and even with inveracity; but these are subsidiary charges; individual anglers may or may not have to plead guilty to them. The charge of cruelty admits no exceptions. We may fish in moderation; we may neglect no duty; we may practise fishing as an aid to the performance of duty; we may report the weight of the big fish with mathematical accuracy, without making allowance for atmospheric desiccation or for the incredulity of our friends, and yet, if angling be intrinsically cruel, we anglers, all of us, are doing and encouraging what is intrinsically wrong.

Some readers may feel disposed to brush the charge aside without more ado. They like fishing; it never did them any harm; their fathers and grandfathers before them fished; it is in the blood, and there are many worse ways of spending a day. Fishing keeps the lads out of mischief. Why bother about a handful of dismal croakers who cannot catch fish themselves, and grudge us our amusement?

Those who fish and think will not be satisfied with any such reply. The charge of cruelty must be taken seriously; for it is a serious charge. It can be refuted, I believe, but there is a case to meet; and if the case is to be met effectively, we must be prepared to do some close thinking and to make some fine distinctions; it is on those distinctions that the case really turns. The truth here is on a razor-edge. What exactly is cruelty? How does it differ from the infliction of pain? Is all angling defensible? If not, what exactly is the angling here defended? And lastly, what exactly is (or should be) the angler's aim?

The problem, as I see it, is essentially ethical, and not religious; and the main argument of this chapter is conducted in terms of right and wrong, not in terms of precept and prohibition. Therefore the conclusions reached, if sound, ought to be accepted by all who believe in right and wrong, no matter what their religion, and if they have no religion. In Christian countries, however, a rigorously ethical attitude in such a discussion would be impracticable, and many people will think, quite rightly, that the example and precept of Christ and the social code that has resulted from His teaching ought to be very seriously considered in connection with the abstract question of right and wrong, and I will therefore venture a few preliminary remarks on this aspect of the question.

The angler is an accepted member of Christian society. The Christian tradition of centuries has approved of angling in general, and that approval is latent in the law of the land. It is true that this argument does not go the whole way; for Christian practice does not always conform to Christian principle, and, as in the case of slavery, the full implications of Christianity may dawn slowly on the Christian conscience. But there is no parallel between slavery and angling; and it is hard to see how development of thought could radically affect the latter issue. The Gospels contain no precept or prohibition about it. There is no, 'Thou shalt fish', or 'Thou shalt not fish'; but there is evidence of a special consonance between Christianity and fishing.

Christ companied with fishermen; at least seven of His apostles fished. Peter, James and John were partners in fishing. Thomas, the thinker, fished, and so did Nathaniel and two others.* Jesus worked miracles with fish, and often spoke of fish in parables and sermons. He entered in a marked way into the thoughts and feelings of fishermen, and understood their avocation. "Bring of the fish which ye have now caught," He said to the seven fishermen when He called them to breakfast by the shore of the lake. He Himself provided fish with bread and a fire of coals; they, tired and hungry, but proud of their great catch of "great fishes . . . an hundred and fifty and three", wanted to show and share them, as any anglers would. And if anyone objects that the fishing approved in the Gospels was net fishing, and not angling, there are two replies: first, that Peter certainly was an angler, too, and Christ sanctioned his angling, and made use of it, when He bade him cast a hook into the sea, and catch a fish;† second, that in respect of the charge of cruelty the principle is the same, net fishing, if anything, being more open to the charge than angling.

People who feel that Christ might have been merely acquiescing in the practice of the day, and who desire a deeper approach, should consider the attitude to nature, implied in His characteristic sayings. A sparrow "shall not fall on the ground without your Father" (Matthew x, 29). "Your heavenly Father feedeth them" (ibid., vi, 26). "God clothes the grass and decks the lilies of the field" (ibid., vi, 28-30). To take such sayings as mere poetic ornament would take the heart out of them, and would be completely foreign to their context. They imply a sense of the intimate presence of God in nature, and the existence of a Providential Order. The philosopher would say that they spring from the principle of *panentheism*, which holds that all created things are *in* the Creator-Spirit, as the play *Hamlet*, its plot, characters, movement, time, place and staging, were *in* the mind of Shakespeare.‡ There are other sayings, such as,

* John xxi, 2. † Matthew xvii, 27.

‡ Panentheism is on no account to be confused with Pantheism. The two words look alike, but the two systems are at opposite poles of thought. Pantheism teaches that all is God; it has no scale of values, and tends to make physical pain and moral evil illusory. Panentheism distinguishes God from His creation, stresses the scale of values, and accepts the reality of pain and evil.

"Ye are of more value than many sparrows" (ibid., x, 31) and the kindly, almost whimsical question, "Are ye not much better than they?" (ibid., vi, 26), which imply a feature of the Providential Order, of great importance to our purpose, namely, the scale of values. In these great sayings and the Providential Order they depict and voice, Christians learn from childhood their *duties* and their *rights* with regard to birds and beasts and fishes and the flowers of the field. These things with ourselves have their places in the Providential Order, and each is entitled to its measure of respect. God cares for all these things. It is unnatural and un-Christian to shoot sparrows for fun, to pull the legs off spiders wantonly, or even to pull roses to pieces out of spite or petulance. "A righteous man regardeth the life of his beast."* Consideration for animals is part of the *a b c* of Christian duty; but consideration does not require us to be sentimental. We must be kind to dumb animals; but we may use their services. We may not subject them to unnecessary or avoidable pain; but human life stands higher in the scale. Christians *respect* life in all its forms, but they do not *worship* it; and they are authorized by religion and common sense to take animal life where human need requires it; and man's first need is food.

Leaving religion aside, let us now face the ethical question on an ethical basis. Is angling cruel? People with a conscience who love their fishing rod are placed in a sad dilemma, as long as the question remains unanswered; and those who with Izaak Walton "love virtue and angling" will not grudge the time and trouble involved in answering it thoroughly; and no answer but a thorough answer really meets the case.

What we know to be cruel we know to be wrong. If all angling is cruel, then my angling is wrong. There may be those who are prepared to say, "My angling, right or wrong"; but such are few in number. Most men of education recognize that right and wrong have a public aspect, and that amusements in particular mould national character and

* Proverbs xii, 10.

express it. The ethics of bull-fighting is a public question, and so is the ethics of angling. None of us lives to himself in such matters. If we have not the care of children and direct responsibility for their up-bringing, at least we are responsible for the impact of our example upon our set and society; and the thought that we are setting a bad example and encouraging cruelty, whenever we went out for a day on the river, would spoil the day for many of us.

The term 'cruel' is ambiguous; and to fix its meaning in this context is a first essential, if cross-purposes are to be avoided. We deal below with four cases of eminent people who thought angling cruel, or are said to have done so. In one of the cases, for certain, and perhaps in others the root of the trouble was that they had not thought out the precise meaning of the term *cruel*. ***Cruelty is the voluntary infliction of unnecessary or avoidable pain.*** That is the sense in which the word should be used in a discussion of the ethics of angling. Those who call angling a cruel sport, if they are speaking precisely and mean what they say, mean that anglers in their angling voluntarily inflict on fish unnecessary pain. That is the charge which I here endeavour to refute in respect of the properly conducted angling for game fish, traditional in Great Britain and Ireland.

The key points in the foregoing definition of cruelty are the words *voluntary* and *unnecessary*. We speak of the east wind as 'cruel'; but we do not blame the wind for being cruel, any more than we blame a knife for cutting. We call avalanches, earthquakes and hurricanes 'cruel' because they seem inconsistent with the, for the most part, kindly course of nature. But wind, knife, avalanche, earthquake and hurricane are all inanimate things; they cannot *act* in the true sense; they have no volition; they cannot act voluntarily, and therefore the term *cruel*, as the moralist uses it, does not apply to them. They may be unpleasant; they may cause pain; but only voluntary agents can in the strict sense be cruel.

This is an important preliminary, which cuts away a good deal of vague and loose criticism. There can be no cruelty in angling unless it is in the angler. Critics who would hesitate to call anglers cruel men, or men who indulge themselves in cruelty when they go a-angling, do not hesitate to say, 'Well, at any rate, they are taking part in a cruel sport.' Now if those words mean anything — and often they mean very little — they must mean that angling has an unpleasant side to it, which of course is the fact. We must not blink the facts if we wish to get at the truth of the matter. Angling involves pain and death. The angler, *qua* angler, inflicts pain and causes death. People, so constituted by nature that they cannot do those things without revulsion, ought not to angle. That is plain; nor ought they to make the cruel charge of cruelty against all who do them. The pain inflicted by the considerate, humane angler is very slight, for the most part, as I shall show, and very brief. Pain and death come to all living things; and death at the angler's hand, if he lives up to the sportsman's traditional code, is in almost all cases more merciful, quicker and less painful than death in other forms, including death from 'natural causes' — if there is such a thing in the fish-world.*

The other key point in the definition of cruelty is the word *unnecessary* or *avoidable*. The infliction of pain *per se* does not constitute cruelty. Surgeon and dentist and minister of justice have to inflict pain in the course of their duties. Butchers have to inflict death in the course of the day's work. No one would dream of calling those avocations cruel, or the men who perform them, cruel, provided no unnecessary pain is inflicted. Angling implies the infliction of a small amount of pain, and death; but so does almost every meal we hungry mortals take. If the critic is to establish his charge of cruelty against angling, as such, he must be in a position to show that all forms of angling involve the infliction of wanton or unnecessary pain; and that cannot be shown of the traditional angling for salmon and trout, conducted by fair methods, in the right spirit and for the right object.

* It is very rare to find a dead or dying trout; if one asks the reason why, and allows the imagination to reply, one sees the truth and feels the force of the foregoing observation.

We will glance now at the opinions of those who think angling a cruel sport. Even those, like the writer, who do not agree with them can learn much from them. We may indignantly repudiate the charge of cruelty and yet be grateful to our critics who raise the question and argue it fairly; they may be doing a public service; for there is a cruel streak in most men; there are cruel tendencies in innocent occupations. We need to be reminded of these facts, and those who sound the Alert deserve our thanks. Some critics indeed are not helpful; they are warm-hearted, sympathetic folk, guided more by the heart than the head. They imagine themselves on a hook at the end of a line, struggling for dear life in deep water; and they let that image settle the question for them. People who feel that way have not the robustness that an angler needs; they ought not to angle or read books on angling; angling is not for them. Anglers can respect their scruples, without feeling bound by them. We, too, have scruples; anglers yield to no class of society in respect for the moral law. Most of us hate cruelty. Angling, done in the right spirit, makes men sensitive and thoughtful. Anglers are in hourly touch with kindly nature. Their occupation is solitary often, but never lonely; they have time for the higher Presences; they have time to study and know themselves; they have time to learn the general features of the world in which they fish and think awhile. This chapter is not an all-out defence of all forms of angling; nor is it an attack on all critics of angling. It is written to help men of two loves. It is written for those who love virtue and angling, who believe that there is no lasting disharmony or discord between those two loves, and who desire an intellectual confirmation of that belief.

In his book of angling reminiscences, recently published, *My Rod, My Comfort*,* Sir Robert Bruce Lockhart, K.C.M.G., the distinguished diplomat and author, names Lord Byron, Robert Louis Stevenson and Thomas Masaryk as men who thought angling cruel, and he associates *himself* with the charge. The four cases differ slightly. Stevenson and

* London, 1957.

Masaryk gave up angling; the other two apparently did not. I discuss the four cases separately, and hope that the discussion will bring out the essential points in a critical defence of the morality of angling.

Lord Byron in a satire on various occupations wrote as follows:

> And angling too, that solitary vice,
> Whatever Izaak Walton sings or says,
> The quaint old, cruel coxcomb in his gullet
> Should have a hook, and a small trout to pull it.*

In a footnote on the stanza Byron adds, "It would have taught him humanity at least. This sentimental savage whom it is a mode to quote (amongst the novelists) to show their sympathy for innocent sports and old songs, teaches how to sew up frogs, and break their legs by way of experiment, in addition to the art of angling — the cruellest, the coldest and the stupidest of pretended sports. They may talk about the beauties of nature, but the angler merely thinks of his dish of fish . . . even net fishing, trawling, etc., are more humane and useful. But angling! No angler can be a good man."

A note on the above footnote states, "One of the best men I ever knew . . . was an angler," and Byron adds, "The above addition was made by a friend in reading over the MSS. *Audi alteram partem.* I leave it to counter-balance my own observations."

Byron had experience in certain forms of fishing; for he wrote to a friend, "I have caught a great many perch and some carp, which is a comfort as one would not lose one's labour willingly."† How far he would wish us to take seriously his attack on angling is hard to say. As a poet he had penned an amusing, but extravagant, conceit, and as a man he had to justify it. By his own admission the passage is overdrawn and unbalanced. If a man finds angling cold,‡ he should not fish early in the season; if he finds it stupid,

* *Don Juan*, Canto XIII, cvi.
† *Letters and Journals*, vol. III, p. 131. The letter is dated 7 September, 1814.
‡ I have taken the term literally. Possibly Byron meant 'cold-blooded', a synonym for 'cruel'.

he is a bad scholar, and if he finds it cruel, the cruelty is of his own making.

Byron's attack on the cruelty of Walton's 'minor tactics' is more to the point and more serious. Honesty requires that the passage should be quoted, but it goes against the grain with me to quote them. The words bear out what was said above (p. 176) about the cruel streak in man. No angler today would justify openly Walton's treatment of the frog (though such things are done still), but it needs to be remembered to Walton's credit that if the standard of sportsmanship has risen since his day, and if we are in a position to criticize some few of his methods, that is largely because of his own gracious thinking and gracious writing. He wrote beautifully about angling in ugly times; in the midst of the civil war he wrote of angling with calm and peace of mind. He raised the tone and spirit of angling for all who will to be *compleat* anglers. If Izaak Walton found angling a sport, he left it an art, an active contemplation, and a recreation of mind and morale. After three centuries many of his sayings lend wings to the rising soul.

Robert Louis Stevenson, in a letter dated 13 July, 1894, gives a vivid picture of the incident that put an end to his fishing. He had always been accustomed, he says, laboriously to kill every fish as he took it, but one day in 1871 "in the Queen's river I took so good a basket that I forgot those niceties, and when I sat down in a hard rain shower under a bank to take my sandwiches and sherry, lo and behold, there was the basketful of trouts still kicking in their agony. I had a very unpleasant conversation with my conscience. All that afternoon I persevered in fishing, brought home my basket in triumph, and sometime that night 'in the wee sma' hours ayont the twal' I finally forswore the gentle craft of fishing." If he made up his mind that angling was cruel, he does not say so here. He had sinned against the first law of angling sportsmanship; he had been cruel, and he had a bad time with his conscience, and he deserved it. The account reads more like a personal act of contrition than as a moral judgment on the ethics of angling. He was exceptionally delicate, physically and mentally; his constitution lacked (fortunately for our heritage of letters) an angler's toughness of fibre, and he was right to give up angling. The incident is a useful warning against cruelty by neglect; but there is nothing in it, or in Stevenson's words or example, to warrant an adverse verdict on the ethics of angling in general.

Thomas Masaryk's case must be treated at greater length; it illustrates the importance of having a clear view of the primary *object* of angling; for this is the key point in the ethical problem. Masaryk is described by Sir Robert Bruce Lockhart as "the gentle sage of Czechoslovakia who first taught his countrymen to catch fish with fly".* He was a keen angler, and he wrote the memorable words, "Wherever there are trout, it is always beautiful." He loved trout so much that he could not kill them, and when he caught them he put them back in the water. It was an amiable trait in his character; but when you study the principle involved, and universalize it (as Kant would say), you see that the principle of such angling is wrong, and that it opens the door for more serious abuses. The value of Masaryk's testimony on the charge of cruelty is *nil*; for *his* angling was cruel, and is not the angling here defended.

Masaryk married, and his wife persuaded him, we are told, to give up fishing altogether; "she was so sorry for the fish". She was quite right; she was right to be sorry for the fish, and right to put a stop to angling of that sort. To hook trout and put them back into the water, unless they are too small to keep and quite uninjured, is to inflict pain, however small the amount, unnecessarily, and it therefore comes under the definition of cruelty. It is a mild form of cruelty; but it is cruelty; it involves the infliction of pain without the hunter's justification for doing so. Approve it; practise it, and you are estopped from disapproving and trying to end the harsher forms. If the statesman-angler had brought home a nice basket of trout, his wife would have had no case, and probably she would have encouraged him to continue fishing.

* op. cit., p. 17.

It may look paradoxical at first sight to hold that it is cruel to hook and release trout, and not cruel to hook and kill them; but such is the case. Cruelty is largely in the mind and motive, and it is just here that the primary object of angling becomes of importance for both theory and practice.

The primary object of justifiable angling is to catch fish for food; there are various pleasures incidental to angling; but they cannot justify the infliction of pain or death.

Masaryk was not interested in trout as food. Why then did he fish? No doubt he enjoyed the fresh air and exercise and the change of occupation, as we all do; but those delights may easily be had without the aid of a fishing rod. If his object was practice in casting, why did he not cast at a cork on the water, or at a hoop on the ground as they do in casting competitions? But, no. Masaryk took his rod and went out for a day's trouting, and caught trout; but he did not keep them; he did not want to keep them; he was not interested in them as wholesome food; and one is driven to the conclusion that he was interested in them merely as animated targets. He did not want them to suffer; but he enjoyed himself at their expense; and he got pleasure out of their pain and fright. He did not wish them to suffer; but they suffered, and he had the artist's pleasure in *expertise*. On the evidence it looks as if the primary aim and object of his angling was the pleasure of cultivating, practising and displaying the art of casting. He fished for pleasure, and not, strictly, for fish; therefore his angling was, I submit, in principle, unethical.

I do not wish to make a mountain out of a molehill, much less to smear a well-intentioned action by a good and kindly man; but he made a mistake in judgment. This is a case where the truth is on the razor-edge; and it is a moralist's duty to bring the truth to light.

What is the angler's aim, *qua* angler? Should he fish for fish or fish for pleasure? It is a fine point, I grant, that at first sight appears finicking, and it can easily be ridiculed; but it is a turning-point in theory; and in practice it may have far-reaching consequences. Once grant that it is right to catch fish for pleasure, or amusement, or sport, and it becomes very difficult to draw any consistent line that will exclude massive forms of cruelty to animals. Here is a story, founded on fact, that may help to illustrate the difference between the primary object of an action, and the accompanying feelings.

Doctor Brown, a specialist in ethics and a confirmed angler, delivered a lecture on *Motives* at a clerical meeting in the west of Ireland. The Archdeacon was in the chair. The lecture was an all-out attack on hedonism. Pleasure, said the Doctor, is not the test of right and wrong; it is not the universal motive; it is scarcely to be called a motive at all. If we want to *get* pleasure, we must *forget* it. Pleasure, like health, is best attained when least thought of; men seek pleasant objects; but only rarely, if at all, do they seek the feeling of pleasure. If they say they do a thing for pleasure, it is a sure sign that they have not thought out what their real motive is. He instanced angling. The true angler, said the Doctor, fishes for fish, and not for pleasure. His primary object, as angler, is to catch fish under sportsman's conditions in order to supply his larder and increase the nation's food supply. He will get the pleasure of angling only if he forgets it. It is pleasant, as a French novelist wrote, to cast the long, rippling, delusive line and ponder the infinities; it is pleasant to hear the rare song of the water-ouzel in the springtime, and to see the royal blue of the kingfisher, flashing by; it is pleasant to escape from city life a while and get fresh air and exercise by the river's brim; but if the angler goes a-fishing with the *object* of getting these pleasant feelings, he will probably miss them, and he will come home frustrated.

The gaitered Archdeacon listened attentively. He was a man of affairs, a typical *oculus episcopi*. He had no patience with fine-spun academic distinctions; philosophy and ethics were lost on him; but he did understand about the fishing, or thought he did. For he, too, was a keen angler, and when he had done his duty by the temporalities of the diocese and the spiritualities of his city parish, he was wont to steal away to the river, and catch a trout or two. In his summing-up at the end of the lecture the Archdeacon thanked the Doctor for his able and interesting discourse. "I agree with all of it," he said; "I agree with all of it, except about the fishing. There I venture to disagree with the learned Doctor; for I do fish for pleasure; and, what's more, so does he." (Cheers, and laughter.)

"A hit, a palpable hit." The Archdeacon went home, encouraged by the applause; he brushed up his *Compleat Angler*, wrote a neat little poem in the Izaak Walton manner, and inserted it in the next number of the Diocesan Magazine after the report of the Clerical Meeting: the Doctor bids his scholar to put away his books, and come out for a day on the river, carefully explaining to the young man that they were going out to catch fish, and not to get pleasure.

> They went and fished till on the bank
> The speckled beauties lay in rank;
> A gleam suffused the Doctor's eyes,
> A gleam of proud and glad surprise;
> It caught the student's dancing eyes . . .

That was the point of the poem; the gleam in the Doctor's eyes was supposed to belie his statement that he did not fish for pleasure. The Archdeacon thought he had scored a bull; in fact he was off the target altogether.

The Doctor did his best to point this out. In the next number of the Magazine he replied in rather ponderous verse, making clear the essential points of his thesis.

He wrote:

> I go a-fishing in due measure,
> An apostolic use of leisure.
> I grant it is my earnest wish,
> My keen delight, to hook a fish.
>
> And yet, my scholar, do not doubt,
> I simply go to fish for trout.
> For if I went to fish for pleasure,
> I'ld miss it, and the speckled treasure.

For Pleasure is the lady coy,
  Teasing her faithful shepherd boy;
Seek Pleasure, and she loves to flout;
  Forget her, and she seeks you out.

Be taught then by the piscatorial game
  The difference 'twixt true and fancied aim;
And take this moral from the art of creeling:
  Just do your job, and never mind the feeling.

The last stanza was happily turned by the late Sir Robert Tate, K.B.E., an angler who loved Latinity, thus:

Est aliud quod vis, aliud quod velle videris;
  Talia piscator te meminisse docet.
Accipe, "fiat opus" tibi si praeceperit idem,
  Neu tibi quid placeat displiceatve roga.

Just do your job, angler. *Fiat opus.* Get on with the good work. Catch the eatable fish by sportsman's methods. Administer the *coup de grâce* without delay; and no one can throw a stone at you on the score of morals. You are not being cruel. You are not causing unnecessary pain. There is pleasure in the pastime, of course. Few would fish if it were otherwise. The artistry of angling, the sportsman's wiles, intelligence pitted against instinct, the fresh air, the open spaces, and the change of scene and occupation — these are all part of the joy of angling, blameless, pleasurable elements in the sportsman's pursuit of fish; but our *pleasure* is not the proper object of our angling, and it could not *per se* justify the suffering and death we inflict and cause. How then can they be justified?

"Beast of the earth . . . fowl of the air . . . fishes of the sea . . . every moving thing that liveth shall be meat for you."* Those verses give the primal permission to kill for food; they voice in the language of religion what in other contexts could be called the biological law of life through death. A scale of values runs throughout the whole field of life, proving the upward *nisus* of evolutionary trends; the lower dies that the higher may live. Man has a right to kill

* Genesis ix, 2, 3.

for food. It is the law of God. It is the law of nature. It is the law of God in nature, defining an ultimate condition of human life. Man has a right and duty to kill for food. As long as angling keeps within the limits of that right, it is blameless, and the charge of cruelty fails; for the pain incidental to the act of killing for food has to be accepted as an unavoidable part of the present scheme of things; the problem of pain is acute and at times distressing to the thinker; religion and philosophy can help to ease it; the fact of pain cannot be avoided. The right to kill for food, however, does not confer the right to kill for fun, or amusement, or sport, or pleasure. It does not confer the right to cause unnecessary pain; and the duty of reducing the sufferings of fish, and of making the death pang brief and merciful is Article No. 1 in the angler's code of honour.

There are one or two minor points to be cleared up here; for some readers perhaps are feeling that the foregoing justification of angling may answer some objections, but does not touch the spot; they think it takes the sport out of angling, and makes it a business, and does not correspond to fact; for the simple reason that we anglers do not fish for food.

Take this last point first. The table qualities of salmon and trout are not actually present to our minds when we are fishing; we do not fish for food in that sense. We do not often have to fish to get food. None the less we do fish *for what is food*, and we do not fish, save *per accidens*, *for what is not food.* Those facts make all the difference when the morality of our angling is challenged. Predators destroy food, and have therefore to be destroyed; but it is extremely difficult to justify the killing of harmless *uneatable* fish.*

* That the edibility of the fish has much to say to the morality of angling for them is confirmed by one's instinctive reactions to the capture of pike and perch. A self-observant angler is bound to notice how differently he feels towards them. He cannot help catching them at times when trolling; but they are a nuisance to him in more ways than one; they are a psychological nuisance to him when he sees them lying dead on the floor-boards; they offend his eye; they are 'kills'; but they are not what he came to get; they are not the proper objects of his angling.

Pike and perch, of course, are not absolutely uneatable; but few sportsmen eat them. They have better fish to fry.

As for the charge of turning a sport into a business, true sportsmen will always treat angling as a liberal occupation, and are not in the least likely to commercialize it. True, the moral justification for angling is the same as that for commercial fishing, namely man's right to kill for food; but that fact does not require the angler to lower his aim and fish to make money. We all desire and value sportsmanship in our angling; the carefree spirit of sport is not so desirable. Sportsmanship guarantees fairness, mercy, kindness and consideration for man and animal, for gillie and for fish; the sporting spirit does not always do so. Angling is not a sport like cricket and football; for angling involves the infliction of pain and death, and cricket and football do not. Angling has a psychological basis in the hunting instinct; that is why it appeals so strongly to many folk; and that is why its tendencies need watching. If in accordance with usage we call angling a sport, we certainly ought not to practise it as a sport. We cannot sport with the lives of God's living creatures as we sport with a lifeless ball; if we do so, if we inflict pain and death light-heartedly without regard for the lives and feelings of trout, the charge of cruelty would come unpleasantly near the truth.

Here is a summary of the foregoing argument:

> ***The pleasures of angling explain why people angle; but the proper defence of the morality of our traditional sporting angling for game fish,* and the angler's justification for taking life and inflicting pain, have nothing to do with the angler's pleasure. The defence and the justification are simply that the angler is killing fish for food.***

The foregoing argument was drafted a stone's throw from the lake in full view of fishing boats and rods and anglers, and any critic who feels disposed to write off the argument as 'academic' should stop and inquire the meaning of that overworked term. There was some excuse for using it as the equivalent of 'abstract' or 'remote from reality' when

* Not having had any experience of other types of angling I do not presume to speak of them.

College dons lived cloistered lives in academic groves. In university life today cloisters and groves are rare, and the dons, like cobblers, stick to their lasts, and leave it to other members of the community to pontificate without experience. Personally I should be ashamed to advance a serious argument that was unacademic and unworthy of university thought. To me an 'academic' argument is one that is clear and unambiguous, precise and exact, and in touch with the realities of the situation, and I sincerely hope that the foregoing argument will be found 'academic' in that sense.

For those who find it too exact or too precise, or who for any other reason cannot follow it, let me add a second-best argument that has some claim to be called 'popular'. It is sometimes advanced as a defence of the morality of angling; and it is a partial answer to certain charges that the angler must face. We may call it the 'balance of pleasure' argument. In a nutshell it is this: Angling gives a great deal of pleasure to the angler, and does him good in body, mind and spirit. It may cause a little extra pain and suffering in the fish world; but when a balance is struck, the preponderance of additional pleasure is so great that angling is empirically justified by its results.

This line of defence is better than no defence at all. The notion of a balance of pleasure is at least a principle, and an inferior principle of action is better than action without any principle at all. The angler who acts on this principle will be constantly reminded that fish suffer, and that it is his duty to shorten and reduce their sufferings. There is also some worldly wisdom in the notion, and it is a useful answer to the sentimentalist who exaggerates the sufferings of fish. Still the 'balance of pleasure' principle sheds very little light on the angler's path; it does not help in a case of conscience. When Robert Louis Stevenson was having a bad time "in the wee sma' hours" about the "trouts still kicking in their agony", it would not have helped him to remember how much he enjoyed the sherry and sandwiches and the elation of piscatorial success.

The 'balance of pleasure' is very much a second-best

argument; it belongs to a lower plane of ethical thought. Obviously there is no measuring-rod; there is no hedonic calculus that can reckon man's pleasure against trout's pain. Two can be added to two, and one can be taken away; but two pleasures cannot be added together, nor can a pain be subtracted from the sum. Our moral intuitions lie too deep for arithmetical calculation. Right and wrong can never be explained in terms of pleasure and pain. Cruelty is cruelty, no matter who is pleased. Cruelty is wrong, no matter what is gained.

We pass on now to a third line of defence, if defence it can be called; it amounts, in my view, to throwing up the case, and refusing to recognize the court. We have discussed the views of Byron, Stevenson and Masaryk, and in the course of the discussion we have reached principles which my companions of the rod will feel, I hope, as a satisfactory defence of the morality of angling and as a refutation of the general charge of cruelty. It remains to consider the strange position in the matter taken up by Sir Robert Bruce Lockhart, whose recent book introduced the subject here discussed. After mentioning that these three great men thought angling cruel, he wrote, "I shall not attempt to defend the charge of cruelty. Nature is cruel and man is its child."* Those words, taken seriously, amount in their context to saying, "Yes, as Byron, Stevenson and Masaryk held, fishing is cruel; and I cannot answer them; but I have fished, and shall fish; for Mother Nature is cruel, and I am her child."

Some anglers might defend angling, or try to defend it, along those lines and the sentiment must be examined with care; but to regard the words quoted as Sir Robert's considered opinion is difficult; for they are inconsistent with the tone and tenor of the rest of his book; they are an *obiter dictum*, I think, a passing remark, imperfectly thought out and illogically† expressed. His rod has been his comfort; that were a psychological impossibility, had his angling been cruel.

* op. cit., p. 17.

† The phrase 'its child' is illogical. By personifying Nature we can speak of man as 'her child'. Neuter 'nature' has no children.

Sir Robert expressly dissociates himself from "godless materialism".* He clearly believes in spirit and moral values; he thinks of human affairs with understanding, and writes of them with a kindly and delicate touch. That a man of high principle who weighs his words should seriously regard angling as cruel, and yet remain an unrepentant angler is improbable; that such a one should write a book in praise of angling is incredible. I take Sir Robert's *dictum* to be an epigram, almost a paradox, and not more. Still he has said it in public. He has conceded that angling is cruel, and has attempted to justify the cruelty by a far-reaching and pessimistic statement about nature. An answer is called for.

Sir Robert's epigram and the smart philosophizing behind it remind one of Common Room chatter *after* Commons. I overheard the following conversation some years ago between the pale-faced pessimist of the Common Room and his friend, the bronzed angler. The pessimist was sipping his vintage port after a good dinner on salmon mayonnaise, and between sips he asked for trouble, and got it:

Pessimist: "Where did you get that complexion, James?"

Bronzed Angler: "I've been fishing for a fortnight on the lake."

Pessimist: "Murdering those gentle trout? You're a blood-sport addict, you are. You should see a psychiatrist, James, or a parson."

Bronzed Angler: "You seemed mighty happy with your slice of middle-cut just now, Charles; and do you know, my tender-hearted friend, that one of your 'gentle trout' murders one thousand flies a day, and has been seen at it? I belong to the N.S.P.C.F., the National Society for the Prevention of Cruelty to Flies. That's why I kill trout."

The Common Room enjoys repartee, especially *after* Commons, and does not take it too seriously; but there is something more than repartee, something approaching solid argument in the Bronzed Angler's retort. It is roughly true

* op. cit., p. 72.

that the angler kills trout, as the trout kills flies, and therefore that the trout are but getting what they give. Lord Bacon* speaks of 'wild justice' and the appeal to some sort of wild or rough justice is common to the Angler's retort and to Sir Robert's epigram. That is the grain of truth in both remarks. Sir Robert is wrong, however, in taking 'wild justice' to be cruelty. The trout is not *cruel* to the fly; the trout takes the fly for food, as the angler takes the trout for food. We may call it sternness or justice, but it is not cruelty. There is no cruelty, properly so-called, implied or involved. It is the rarest thing to find deliberate or wanton cruelty in the animal world. The course of nature is just; it may be stern, but it is never cruel. Nature herself is not cruel, and nothing that Nature does, or is, confers on man a licence to be cruel. What we know to be cruel, we know to be against nature, unnatural and wrong.

We should hate to think that Nature is cruel, when our time comes to reel up and pay the universal debt of nature; why not take the saner and sounder view while we are in full enjoyment of Nature's loan of life? It is true that pain and suffering and death are found over a wide area of existence; but pleasure and happiness, peace, achievement and life are found over a much wider area. Pessimists are mesmerized by the negative aspect of evolution; they forget that evolution posits and creates. They look at the struggle for existence; they see the incessant competition for food, for mate and for living-space; and they overlook the settled coexistence of the main forms of life, the balanced order of species, and the ceaseless struggle by individuals for the life of others. Frown at Nature, and she frowns back. Smile, and she answers with a smile. Nature is "red in tooth and claw" for those only who wish to see her so, who refuse to meet her smiling eyes, who have never felt her healing touch in sickness, who have never watched her patience with our weakness, who never ponder her serene wisdom and the queenly bounty of her giving and forgiving.

Animals suffer and feel pain, *pace* Descartes. The plea,

* "Revenge is a kind of wild justice." *Essay on Revenge.*

sometimes advanced, that dumb fishes do not feel pain cannot be sustained. Fish undoubtedly suffer, and only the cruel or callous will be indifferent to their sufferings. At the same time it is foolish to go to the opposite extreme, and imagine that they feel the pain that we should feel in their place. They obviously do not. Man looks before and after and above; he expects, remembers and aspires. He has reason, speech, laughter and tears, a central core of feeling, and the fabric of higher selfhood. The trout has none of these things; the pain he feels is probably at a low degree of sensitivity; it may be like the pain we feel in twilight consciousness when we come round after an anaesthetic. On well-fished waters trout are probably pricked by the artificial fly two or three times a day, and their fear soon passes.

John came in late for lunch with his waders on, and I asked if he had had any luck; he replied, "No; I fished a Coachman dry in that run below the bridge at Foxford opposite the mill. A two-pound trout took me, and broke me." John went back to the same place for the evening rise; he came back at dusk, and displayed the two-pound trout with the morning's Coachman stuck in the side of its mouth. We need not be sentimental about animal suffering; but we dare not be callous or cruel; fish do suffer.

It is a great mistake, however, to allow animal suffering or human suffering to get on our nerves, and to warp our view of the universe. After all, life *is* suffering; life is a rhythm of pleasure and pain, a pendulum-swing from pleasant consciousness to painful consciousness, with a neutral point midway. No one of us could will to lose our pain nerves, or opt for an anaesthetized existence. Life is suffering, but life is good. The very struggle for existence proves that life is good. Man and animal struggle for the life of their kind, and man bears a special testimony to the goodness of life by his undying hope of a personal future life. How can we in fairness charge nature with cruelty when she gives us that life we so earnestly desire. Life involves suffering. Life here and now involves pain and death.

Nature must be stern, but she is stern with the sternness of justice, not of cruelty.

And Nature is merciful. Even death may be a mercy on the long view. Pain is often protective, often remedial, often a blessing in disguise. The wind is tempered to the shorn lamb, and pain in its quality, intensity and duration is usually proportioned to the back that bears it. Great pain brings its own anodyne, unconsciousness; and in spite of the sharpness of birth and death practically everything that lives blesses Nature for her gift of life.

People mean different things by the word 'Nature'; some personify Nature; for some, Nature is an impersonal symbol; for some, Nature is an active force; for others, Nature is passive being; for some, Nature means God; for others, not.* But whatever meaning we attach to the term, it is not true that Nature is cruel; and therefore it cannot be true that Nature sets a headline for man's cruelty.

Angling need not be cruel. Angling, properly conducted in the spirit of Christian sportsmanship, is not cruel. If there are cruel forms of angling, if there are cruel practices or cruel tendencies in angling, the anglers concerned cannot plead by way of justification that Nature is cruel and that they in being cruel are but acting as their mother's sons.

Traditional angling for trout and salmon teaches kindness to animals, shows the need for it, and offers a field for cultivating it. Thoughtful angling should strengthen *morale*, and not weaken it. He who fishes in the right way and thinks along right lines can hardly fail to absorb a healthy moral optimism about Nature and her ways. For Nature does nothing idly, makes nothing bad or ugly, and in sternness remembers mercy. The same can be said in the warmer, and no less truthful, language of religion. Anglers see at close range and in great detail the works and wonders of the Lord. All His works are good. He has made everything beautiful in His time, and His tender mercies are over all His works.†

* To the philosopher the two proper meanings are those defined by the scholastics as (1) *Natura naturans*, i.e., God, as creative spirit, and (2) *Natura naturata*, i.e., the works of God, the created world.

† Genesis, i, 31; Ecclesiastes, iii, 11; Psalms, cxlv, 9.